William Shakespeare

King Lear

Terence Hawkes

Northcote House

in association with
The British Council

To Ann, as ever

Order No:

Class: 822·33

Accession No: 049197

Type: L

British Library Cataloguing-in-Publication Data
A catalogue record for this book is available from the British Library

ISBN 0 7463 0746 2

Typeset by Kestrel Data, Exeter
Printed and bound in the United Kingdom by BPC Wheatons Ltd, Exeter

Contents

Illustrations

The author and the publishers are grateful to the Shakespeare Birthplace Trust for permission to reproduce the stills from past Royal Shakespeare Company productions, which appear in the section between pages 31 and 32.

Preface

What follows is not meant to be a systematic account of *King Lear*, nor an objective survey of different approaches to it. The subject is too vast for that, and the amount of critical writing the play attracts increases daily at a pace well in excess of the most dedicated efforts at mastery. It consists, rather, of a series of proposals, presented as individual chapters and angled in different directions, which might form the basis for a linked group of seminar discussions on the play. The sense that there is far more to say about *King Lear* than has been set down here is inherent in any such project, where the single voice that is heard presupposes the many that are not.

I have tried in the main to keep to fairly well-trodden paths before venturing down others that may be less well known, but this of course does not mean that much more than a fraction of the relevant ground has been covered. But I have tried to ensure, as I do with my own students, that a certain level of self-awareness is nevertheless maintained: that the sort of critical analysis proposed and put to use here should itself from time to time be examined and assessed in the light of its relation to other, possibly less obtrusive but no less influential, procedures.

At the points where this is done, particularly in connection with various uses of history as proposed in Chapters 2 and 9, I hope that I have made clear what my own prejudices, presuppositions, and preferences are. I trust that others will, in opposition, feel able to do the same. Labels, such as those of New Historicism and Cultural Materialism, do not absolve us from the responsibility of a constant re-examination of the positions they purport to describe. The – to me – liberating proposal that there is, in the end, no essential *King Lear*, no play *in itself*, comes with the challenge that there can be no ready-made, no transparent, and above all no innocent criticism of it either.

Acknowledgements

That some of the ideas proposed here began life in quite different surroundings is inevitable, but perhaps not undesirable: recurrence is the soil from which revelation grows. I am therefore indebted to my students at Cardiff who, over the years, have sat – and occasionally slept – through many tentative stabs at what follows. Their questions and comments, even their occasional snores, have proved a useful corrective to any hopes I may fleetingly have entertained as to the conclusive nature of my observations. I am also grateful to that broader range of students in a number of different countries on whom, through the agency of the British Council, I have been able to try out earlier versions of similar arguments. That they deserved better goes without saying. Although I dare not claim that this volume supplies it, the series in which it appears offers an appropriate platform from which to thank them. Thanks are also due to my research student, Philip Armstrong, whose vigilant reading of the typescript saved me from a number of errors. Those that persist are of course my own. Small portions of the material have, I hope, gained a good deal from initial airings given elsewhere. I am, none the less, grateful for the opportunity to refashion, recast, and even immodestly repeat occasional sentences and paragraphs. My greatest debt remains – a matter of constant and fully justified repetition – to my wife.

Note on the Text

All references to *King Lear* are to the Arden edition of the play, edited by Kenneth Muir (London: Methuen (Routledge), 1952; rev. 1985).

1

Ruling and Loving

He certainly looks the part. There is the sound of a 'sennet' or an expectant flourish played on a trumpet. Perhaps the great State Throne is hastily dragged into place at the centre of the stage. A servant enters, bearing a small crown. And then, issuing orders as he advances, 'Attend the Lords of France and Burgundy, Gloucester' (I. i. 34) and followed by a crowd of attendants, dukes, and his three daughters, the king appears.

He is old, but far from feeble, and evidently in full command. In fact, his ceremonial robes, the orb and sceptre that he carries, the larger, jewelled crown that he wears, all seem to lend grandeur to his age, even as they confirm it. The minor business completed, Lear turns first to survey, and then address, his court. If he looks like a king, the authoritative tones and the measured style now ensure that he sounds like one too. A respectful and, later, shocked silence falls as he starts to unveil a massive, and hitherto unrevealed project, in which the assertion of the royal plural insists on his own unchallengeable status. For with the courtier Gloucester's meekly compliant 'I shall, my Liege' (I. i. 35) still hanging in the air, Lear immediately and forcefully proceeds to override it with an announcement of his own menacing priorities: 'Meantime, we shall express our darker purpose' (I. i. 36).

Few plays are more disturbing, often inexplicably so, than *King Lear*. And yet few begin with a more clear-cut demonstration and apparent endorsement of the settled majesty and power of kingship as this was perceived in Western Europe from the Middle Ages right through to the seventeenth century, or what is now usually termed the early modern period. It is appropriate that *King Lear* begins in this way, because it turns out that questions concerning the nature of kingship, and the scope of its responsibilities, lie at the centre of the play and inhabit the very fibres of its language. As we shall see, they crystallize in the next words that Lear utters; words that could be said to constitute the very fulcrum on which the play's action turns:

> Give me the map there. Know that we have divided
> In three our kingdom . . .

(I. i. 37–8)

In order to grasp the truly shocking nature of this proposal, it is necessary first of all to try to set the play in its own historical context. At its simplest, the medieval theory of kingship in which the play's original audience had long been steeped presented the monarch as the embodiment of unity. Socially, politically, and spiritually, the king acted as a kind of lynch-pin for the society over which he ruled, bringing to and guaranteeing for it a high degree of order, stability, and coherence. Yet here is a monarch in fact proposing just the opposite role for himself. Lear's 'darker purpose' involves nothing less than division, the drawing of boundaries, the parcelling up of his own country.

Adding to the shock would be the audience's awareness of the events of the recent past. Following the death of Elizabeth, the person who acceded to the British throne in 1603 was also the king of another country: James the Ist of England had already and quite separately been crowned James VIth of Scotland. The potential instability contained in this situation opened the door to a number of possible dangers, including those of foreign invasion and even civil war. In the face of them, the degree of importance given to the unifying role of the monarch has no better measure than the immediate efforts made by James's propaganda machine to stress the coherence which his presence on the throne of both countries was destined to bring.

The old story of Merlin and his prophecy was revived and given new circulation. This refers to the exploits of the warrior Brutus, who, returning from the siege of Troy, had landed in Britain and had founded a new city called *Troynovant* (i.e. London) on the banks of the Thames. Having established his kingdom, he then proceeded disastrously to divide it between his three sons, thereby creating the separate nations of Wales, England, and Scotland. However, Merlin had prophesied that a second Brutus would eventually appear and reunite the realm which would then be named, in his honour, Great Britain.

James's propaganda cast him precisely in the role of the second Brutus, creative pacifier and reunifier of the entire kingdom and, indeed, its new 'father' – functions that his personal titles *Beati pacifici* and *Parens patriae* sought to reinforce. A crop of astonishing metaphors in this vein came in due course to litter his speeches, all aiming to stress the same factors of agglomeration and indivisibility: 'I am the Husbande and all the whole Isle is my lawful wife: I am the Head, and it is my Body; I am the Shepherd and it is my flocke,' and so on.

The whole process received a timely boost on 5 November 1605 with the discovery – or perhaps invention – of the so-called Gunpowder Plot. This potentially spectacular and certainly imaginative terrorist outrage was designed, it was said, literally to disintegrate, by explosion, the new-found political and social unity of Great Britain. Its perpetrators (so the propaganda went) were a group of Catholics in the pay of foreign powers, and the plot was, of course, appropriately foiled by the quasi-divine intervention of the great Protestant integrator James. His role as national saviour thus confirmed, it was given final sanction by the act of Parliament proclaiming the Union of the two crowns in 1608, a series of events processed by the propagandists – not surprisingly – as 'miraculous'.

In this context, King Lear's proposal to divide his kingdom could prove nothing less than shocking to its first audience, raising as it does spectres of division and disorder thought to be at least quieted, if not long laid to rest. In fact, the proposal can be seen to involve far more than the whim of a foolish old man. At the moment when Lear calls for the map, the play begins to engage with issues of much larger concern. In effect, it starts to focus, not on personality but on politics, and on a whole way of life.

If we were looking for a single word to describe the essence of Lear's divisive proposal it could well be 'reductive'. Lear's project effectively reduces the spiritual, 'unifying' dimension of Kingship to the level of a mere land-owner's project for partition in terms of real-estate brokership. The scheme which has 'divided | In three our kingdom' evidently reduces a political unity to disconnected fractions of the whole (the line-break at the main verb mimicking the process by virtually fracturing the sentence structure). And if we wanted a material symbol for the whole process of diminution involved, it lies close to hand: the map itself.

It is important to remember that the culture from which this play was drawn, and to which it spoke, was in general terms not yet a wholly literate one. However, the term 'illiterate' invokes a modern prejudice and is therefore not appropriate here. Large numbers of people at this time could obviously read and write without difficulty, and indeed the period is one of great artistic activity in exactly this sphere. Yet it is also true that large numbers of people could *not* read or write, and that a considerable proportion of those who could, did not (books were expensive, as were candles to read them by). Not surprisingly, much of the writing of the time manifests what has been termed a significant 'oral residue' still embedded in its style. It is probably more accurate to describe Shakespeare's culture as – in very general terms – 'non-literate' or, better still, 'pre-literate' by comparison with our own.

Oral communication is a highly complex business and obviously involves far more than the uttering of mere words via the mouth. Larger bodily gestures, accents, intonation, inflection, spatial relationships, all form part of any face-to-face use of speech. In a pre-literate culture committed to face-to-face speaking and listening as its primary form of social engagement, the written document, which deals, after all, in a series of marks made on a piece of paper, can seem oddly reductive. We know, from accounts of the meetings of 'explorers' and 'pioneers' with indigenous non-literate peoples, that this is also often the case with maps.

Maps usually purport to be objective, accurate, and impartial texts: faithful reproductions of specific terrains. Yet to the inhabitant of those terrains, who usually have an intimate knowledge of them, they frequently appear to be none of those things. Always, and everywhere, maps are bound to diminish; inevitably, they simplify; they are nothing if not 'unfaithful'. Worse, as our own century knows to its cost, maps are never innocent. They cannot help but be extensions and implementations of the particular political and moral positions of the map-makers. Inevitably, a map will reduce an imprecisely defined, but none the less emotionally charged, sense of 'nationhood' to the merely literal, one-dimensional standing of a piece of paper. This sense of maps as divisive and diminishing, the means whereby sacred

4

spaces may be grossly desecrated, is often strongly and emblematically present in Shakespeare. For instance, in *I Henry IV*, in the memorable scene in which the rebels pore over their maps, unwisely parcelling out in advance their ill-gotten gains (II. i. 69 ff.), Hotspur proposes to alter the course of a river which, serving on the map as a boundary-marker, cuts him off from a valuable piece of land. Intrusive 'mapping' of this sort is clearly labelled here as a culpable violation of Nature and it stands indicted as a crime for which harsh punishment should be, and later is, exacted (II. i. 94 ff.).

It is in this sense that the map placed before Lear and presumably simultaneously exhibited to the audience at his command, 'Give me the map there,' can be said virtually to present to its pre-literate society a whole way of life – its own – grotesquely reduced to and barbarically treated as a mere physical diagram. At this point, the play's project becomes far more complex than the exploration of an individual old man's foolishness. The map helps to push it beyond the range of mere personal psychology, beyond the walls of the theatre, and into the public domain. By linking itself with a number of discourses already circulating within the culture and concerned with matters relating to kingship, government, the coherence of the kingdom, and the like, the play becomes part of the larger social colloquy in which all communities engage. It starts to contribute to the debates and discussions operating in that context, and thus helps to construct the world in which its audience lives. This is why Shakespeare's theatre could quite aptly be called 'The Globe'. This is why, written over its entrance, there could quite reasonably appear the words *Totus Mundus Agit Histrionem* ('All The World's a Stage'). And this is why, performed in it, *King Lear* becomes a play that is, in every sense, 'about' politics.

The point is powerfully reinforced at the moment when the map is produced. It is not, of course, without significance that Goneril's husband is called Albany – the old name for the area which a modern map terms Scotland. It is no less significant that Regan's husband is called Cornwall – the old name for Wales and the West of England. In fact, the divisive and reductive nature of Lear's proposal might be more readily underlined if the parts of the map representing these areas were literally torn from the whole, and handed to each daughter respectively, as they finish speaking: 'Of all these bounds, even from this line to this . . . We make thee lady' (I. i. 63 – 6). That which is offered to Cordelia, a 'third more opulent than your sisters' (I. i. 86) then appears as a cut-down, ragged, violated English remainder, on which Troynovant – or London, the place where the play is now being performed – is clearly and ironically visible.

A literal reduction which mimics a larger one, the destruction of the map is all the more remarkable because it has been brought about in the name of love. The question Lear puts to his daughters focuses precisely on the matter. At first sight it probably seems simple enough:

> Which of you shall we say doth love us most?
> That we our largest bounty may extend
> Where nature doth with merit challenge.

> (I. i. 51–3)

In effect, Lear is asking the child's question, 'how much do you love me?' To us that seems hardly sinister. We could, of course, choose to regard an old man's recourse to such childishness as personally degrading, if not merely pitiful. But, since the whole play turns on the issue, to regard Lear's question solely in that light would be to restrict it to a domestic level, and limit its implications to matters that hardly rise above those of common everyday experience. Yet we have already seen that *King Lear* deals with larger dimensions of life than that: matters which, although they connect vitally with the personal, probe well beyond those 'inward' concerns. Lear's question is a good example of this process, and it illustrates once more the extent to which political issues are woven into the very language that the play uses. 'Which of you shall we say doth love us most? . . .' – the matter seems to depend upon a straightforward use of the word 'love'. But at the time the play was first performed, a secondary usage of the word was also available, and a punning relationship between the two thus became possible, even inevitable.

Primarily, the word 'love' refers to the general area of 'affection', so that 'to love' usually means, then as now, 'to have affection for' something. But the secondary usage of 'love' (deriving from Old English *lofian*, 'praise', as opposed to *lufian*, the basis of the primary one) pointed towards a general area of meaning characterized by the notion of 'assessment', and could thus produce a meaning such as 'to appraise, estimate, or state the price or value of' something. In this, it echoed a 'collision' which took place between the Old French verbs *aimer* (to love) and *esmer* (to reckon or calculate), in which a similar intrusion of one word into another's area of reference can be sensed. In both languages, the possibility of pun exists which, once activated, immediately situates 'love' on the level of calculation, and thus virtually reverses, and so betrays, its meaning. In Christian Europe this reversal has of course a most memorable analogue. It occurs at the moment when Judas Iscariot is asked how much he 'loves' Jesus Christ. The *Towneley* Mystery plays offer an appropriate example, with Pontius Pilate actually putting Lear's question, but in respect of Christ:

> PILATUS. Now, Iudas, sen he shalbe sold,
>   how lowfes thou hym? belyfe let se.

(XX. 238–9)

Judas's reply comes with the full ironic force of which the pun is capable:

> IUDAS. ffor thretty pennys truly told
>   or els may not that bargan be.

(XX. 240–1)

In short, it seems that Lear's insistence on putting a price on love has a potential which, once activated, lifts it well clear of the merely personal and pathetic, establishing it as a betrayal of a crucial sort whose consequences involve disaster on an incalculable scale.

It also, once more, helps us to identify in Lear's acts a recurrent and finally characteristic pattern. A dividing, measuring, weighing, and assessing mode is its central feature. The tearing apart of his country's unity, and the calculation of his daughters' love, both confirm his involvement in and commitment to a huge process of diminution which proceeds by division and quantification. Right at the end of this first scene, trying to persuade Burgundy to take on the now disgraced Cordelia, Lear speaks of her in a way that exactly embodies such a process:

> When she was dear to us we did hold her so,
> But now her price is fallen.

(I. i. 196–7)

Its principles have obviously come to inhabit Lear's language so intimately that they can generate – as part of the insulting reference to Cordelia's 'price' – the appalling double meaning of 'dear' (held in great affection/of high financial cost) almost casually and without overt signalling. Lear's crime – its massive scale compounded by his commanding stature – starts to seem characteristic of an entire way of life here: one which insists on measuring the immeasurable and on assessing price at the expense of value. Quite clearly – perhaps this is what disturbs us most of all – it involves procedures which, by the time the play's first scene is over, have become all-embracing, habitual, and unthinking.

2

Using History

It is worth pausing at this stage to consider the sort of analytic manœuvre that has produced the above reading of the opening of *King Lear* and, to some degree, has enabled us to begin an engagement with its disturbing features. It clearly depends upon a sense of the play's structure, the way in which those dimensions lying beyond the level of the plot and its details are arranged. Such a 'structuralist' approach typifies in one way or another a large number of late-twentieth-century accounts of Shakespeare. In them, the 'characters' and the events of the individual story are perceived as functions of a larger purpose, which makes use of them as part of its own broader commitment to more public themes. The play is then subjected to a kind of X-ray analysis in which its underlying (or overriding) concerns can be made manifest.

Any such account of the *King Lear* story will focus initially on the ancient folk-tale in which a daughter is asked in a variety of odd circumstances to tell her father how much she loves him. A version appears in Geoffrey of Monmouth's *Historia Regum Britanniae*, first published in the twelfth century, and others recur in the 1574 edition of *A Mirror for Magistrates*, in William Warner's *Albion's England* (1586), in Holinshed's *Chronicles of England Scotland and Ireland* (1577), and in Spenser's *Faerie Queene*, Book II (1590). The Gloucester story appears quite separately in Book II of Sidney's *Arcadia*. Yet a structural similarity clearly links both tales and perhaps suggests a basis for some of the play's unsettling features. Both Lear and Gloucester are fathers whose children struggle against each other because of a dispute over inheritance. In each case the children separate into 'good' and 'evil' camps. In the Lear story, Cordelia finds herself pitted against Goneril and Regan; in the Gloucester story, Edgar finds himself opposed by

Edmund. The two 'evil' camps, Goneril and Regan on the one hand, Edmund on the other, later unite and make common cause, almost defeating the forces of the 'good', which, for most of the time, are reviled and falsely accused. A motif of established male, paternal authority, challenged by disaffected children, resented by all, and leading to disastrous and irretrievable conflict, is clearly discernible. So, too, are the questions of succession and inheritance, the issues of who has the right to speak, and whose voices should be listened to. These represent, not insignificantly, the material political problems of a decaying system of kingship. Perhaps the play disturbs us at an even deeper level in the twentieth century because it calls up a story encountered in childhood and nowadays usually associated – at least in Britain – with the apparently inconsequential ceremonies (although they are also full of images of paternal authority) of Christmas: *Cinderella*.

However, the account of *King Lear* given in the previous chapter also relies for its disturbing qualities on more public events, with a fairly precise location in time. Since it invokes history, it can be said to involve a kind of historicism. In fact, a recourse to and engagement with history has, since the 1980s, been the characteristic gesture of a good deal of British and American Shakespearian criticism.

The use of history at stake is nevertheless of a particular sort. The result differs radically from another kind of historicism still dominant on both sides of the Atlantic, which tends to focus on historical material as if it formed a 'background' against which literary texts might profitably be placed before being read. Whilst that procedure seems innocent enough, a series of assumptions propels it towards and finally shapes its conclusions. Chief amongst them is a notion of the literary text as a privileged vehicle of communication, perhaps functioning most fruitfully when located in some kind of historical context, but in the end finally independent of it. A covert distinction between text and context, foreground and background, is evidently smuggled in here on behalf of some further and quite major presuppositions. One of them, by its promotion of the 'literary text', involves a simple projection of the values of our own near-universal literacy on to what I have called the 'pre-literate' past. Another reflects an undeclared investment in a particular view of history which has been moulded by its primary commitment to the academic study of literature.

However, two distinct but related attempts to forge a new role for history in literary criticism have now come to the fore: New Historicism and Cultural Materialism. One of the main concerns of the former is to renegotiate that distinction between foreground and background: to relocate and then reread literary texts in quite a different relation to the other material signifying practices of a culture. As its name suggests, New Historicism's own history also involves a programme of radical readjustment. On the one hand, it represents a reaction against an a-historical or 'idealist' view of the world in which an apparently free-floating and autonomous body of writing called 'literature' serves as the repository of the universal values of a supposedly permanent 'human nature'. On the other, it constitutes a rejection of the presuppositions of a 'history of ideas' which tends to regard literature as a static mirror of its time. Its 'newness' lies precisely in its determination to reposition 'literature' altogether, to perceive literary texts as active constituent *elements* and *aspects* of their time, participants in, not mirrors of it; respondent to and involved with numerous other enterprises, such as the law, marriage, religion, and government, all engaged in the production of 'texts' and, as a result, of the cultural meanings that finally constitute a way of life. And it will see these, and particularly the relations of power which operate between them, as equally determining features in respect of particular societies and their culture. What is involved, in short, is a continuing revisionary project which in the last decade or so has aimed at a reassessment of Shakespeare and Elizabethan drama precisely in terms of its connection with politics.

Fundamentally, this has involved locating the drama in history. First, by reinserting the plays into the cultural history of their own time, by abandoning the modern category of 'literature', and by merging them back into the context of the circulating discourses from which 'English' has prised them, it sets out to judge the degree to which the drama was or was not complicit with the powers of the state that seem to sustain it. A programme of this sort clearly owes something to the work of the French social historian Michel Foucault, and it finally calls, as the American critic Leonard Tennenhouse has argued, for a major 'unthinking' of our own appropriating, segregating procedures; those anaesthetizing means whereby we persistently construct the past in our own image. Particularly at stake are the ways in which we manage, as Tennenhouse puts it, to 'enclose Renaissance culture within our own discourse and thus make it speak our notion of sexuality, the family, and the individual'.[1]

To break through the anaesthetic, such an 'unthinking' suggests, is to see that Shakespeare's plays function as part of a quite different discursive order whose contours, boundaries, and dispositions of experience are hardly likely to match those we nowadays take for granted. They spring from and engage with a world quite distinct from our own – one in which, for instance, literary and political texts have yet to be perceived as necessarily different from one another. Like other contemporaneous texts (the distinctions between them often invented by ourselves), Shakespeare's plays do not inhabit some exclusive aesthetic sphere. On the contrary, they participate politically and socially in their society in terms of their capacity to make sense in and of and for it. They thus take their place in an extensive symbolic field which must also include royal proclamations, folk customs, parliamentary debates, architecture, festivals, music, song, letters, and travellers' reports as aspects of a number of different rhetorical or 'textual' strategies available and consistently utilized for the production of meaning. Clearly such a symbolic field also includes the potent texts that we call maps.

Efforts to distinguish between New Historicism, by and large a phenomenon of the American academic system, and Cultural Materialism, its supposed British counterpart, have to contend with the fact that the two operations appear to occupy quite a lot of common ground. Another American critic, Hugh Grady, sees them both as 'postmodernisms', dealing in a 'decentred' notion of art and speaking to and on behalf of a fragmented 'subject' who creates and perceives it.[2] In addition to the features already mentioned, both seem committed to two fundamental undertakings: first, the abandonment of 'organic unity' as the appropriate model for a culture's ideal condition, as well as the chief aesthetic value to which the practice of art within it should aspire, and, second, the rejection or deconstruction of those binary oppostions which currently determine our own world-view and that of past cultures.

In the place of 'organic unity', both New Historicism and

Cultural Materialism offer a view of cultures as inherently dis-unified structures, characteristically held together at any specific time by tensions between competing interests and different practices. Never static or 'finished', always in process, such arrangements seem permanently to teeter on the edge of dis-integration.

Binary oppositions of course constitute the crucial grounding of the business of cultural meaning and ultimately of identity itself. Our 'agreed' view of the world and of our role in it derives from the construction of specific sets of polar opposites: we are what we oppose. So, an enterprise which undertakes to lay bare (in order to make open to change) the principles of that identity's construction will require fundamental conceptual polarities, such as 'city' and 'country', 'flowers' and 'weeds', 'high culture' and 'popular culture', 'men' and 'women', 'nature' and 'culture', 'moral' and 'immoral', 'lawful' and 'criminal' to be challenged and the relationship of their component parts to be reassessed, if not unpicked. This kind of deconstructive analysis and its major conclusion – that such fundamental oppositions are the temporary products of history, politics, or way of life rather than permanent features of nature – gives a voice to those elements of the society which at a given moment find themselves the disfavoured part-ners in their respective oppositions: the ones condemned, that is, by those constructed polarities, to be marginalized, displaced, subordinated, demonized, repressed, or criminalized.

Both New Historicism and Cultural Materialism tend to present these neglected, discounted aspects of society as, in the last analysis, truly definitive of its nature. Weeds, in this view, stand as the final guarantors of the status of flowers and each is unignorably involved in the role played by the other. The result is an emphatic redrawing of what used to be termed the 'Eliza-bethan World Picture'. This ceases to be the organic, unified Golden Age described – in terms of its 'flowers' – by the British critic E. M. W. Tillyard. Instead it appears – from the perspective of its 'weeds' – as an age of cruelty, imprisonment, and torture; given, like our own, to complex programmes of suppression whereby groups of undesirable persons are effectively marginalized, dehumanized, and alienated. We are, in this sense, what we silence. But in the analyses of New Historicism and Cultural Materialism, the silenced are encouraged to speak.

None the less, crucial differences of emphasis remain. It has become commonplace to say that, in some New Historicist studies, for example, a somewhat positivist or 'objective' recuperation and representation of the past seems at times to be on offer. As a result, the Elizabethan theatre appears virtually to function as an instrument of direct political containment, sanctioned for that purpose by a knowing establishment. Cultural Materialism, on the other hand, seems eager (over-eager, some opponents would have it) to seek out the complexities of potential refusal and rejection embedded in early modern texts and anxious to respond sympathetically to the smallest signs of resistance wherever these may be found. It pursues these quarries, friend and foe seem to agree, with a vigour perhaps born of the more harshly divisive tenor of British life. In general terms, its first principles are certainly rooted in the British commitment and orientation of the work of Raymond Williams. The essence of Williams's position lies in his insistence that all aspects of culture are materially present in the world we inhabit; none enjoys 'ideal' or 'immaterial' status. Culture abides in day-to-day practice: it does not and cannot transcend material economic social and political conditions, and it is vested, not in particular enterprises within a way of life, but in the whole range of activities that make up the way of life itself. 'Culture', that is, involves the entire spectrum of whatever people get up to in concrete terms in the material world.

Like New Historicism, Cultural Materialism declines to privilege literature, or to accord writing any 'transcendent' dimension or quality. It places those activities firmly in the context of the general social process, and thus on a par with the activities of subordinate or marginalized groups. In other words, it takes 'high culture' to be, as the British critics Jonathan Dollimore and Alan Sinfield have described it, just 'one set of signifying practices among others'.[3] Committed, by that notion of 'practice', to the idea that we are involved in the continuous 'making' rather than the discovery of cultural meanings, to what I have elsewhere described as the business of 'meaning by,'[4] such a materialism ultimately perceives culture as volatile, undecided, never complete or 'finished', but always in process; always riven, for example, by tensions between at least three modes of historical development which exist concurrently, and which Williams categorizes as the Emergent, the Dominant, and the Residual.[5]

The central distinction between New Historicism and Cultural Materialism resides in the view each takes of the early modern concern with social and political containment, and the role played in it by the drama and the public theatres. As Dollimore formulates the issue: 'did (Shakespeare's) plays reinforce the dominant order, or do they interrogate it to the point of subversion? According to a rough and ready division, new historicists have inclined to the first view, cultural materialists to the second.'[6] Elsewhere, he comments that 'the two movements have differed over just this: it is new historicism which has been accused of finding too much containment, while cultural materialism has been accused of finding too much subversion'.[7]

However this difference may or may not ultimately be resolved, the fundamental contribution of both Cultural Materialism and New Historicism clearly lies in the perception that, whether it is being reinforced or interrogated, any power that shows itself to be susceptible to either operation can never, by that fact, have been totally embracing or entirely dominant. Never a seamless garment, power can only partly cover the body politic. Resistance to it is, therefore, always theoretically and usually practically possible, even inevitable, and indeed is obviously presupposed by the very existence of strategies of containment.

A drama's interrogation of power will, in turn, require it both to draw upon and adjust its own resources to match whatever forms of subjection it encounters. To take just one example: as part of its everyday operations, the Elizabethan theatre was forced to confront the sumptuary laws of a society which permitted certain modes of dress and prohibited others in order to signify specific rankings amongst its citizens. The theatre's own inherited practice of gender cross-dressing, and indeed the broad nature of its art at large, which required commoners to dress as nobility, even royalty, was bound systematically to conflict with those ways of enforcing gender and class distinctions, bringing them into question and, ultimately, to the point of crisis. It thus found itself inescapably engaged with political domination in that particular material form, and as a result could hardly avoid questioning its authority. For whatever overt statements a play may make, its performance on the Elizabethan stage tacitly and simultaneously also proposes that it is custom, or culture, rather than God, or nature, that separates one class from another, and even male from female. In the early modern period, such ideas were explosive, and a combative literary criticism will obviously seek to point this out.

Of course, Cultural Materialism also recognizes that power can seek to generate subversion for its own ends, in order to make its own task of containment easier. A faked Gunpowder Plot, easily put down, would perhaps have had even greater propaganda value than a genuine one: the systematic stimulation of moral panic to serve an establishment's own ends is an ancient stratagem of rule. However, once installed, a mode of subversion remains willy-nilly available for appropriation, and becomes part of the complex of contending forces which governments must learn to orchestrate. Political and social power is rarely monolithic and never total. Material 'rule' is far more likely to consist of a balance shakily maintained between different, competing elements within the sort of uneasy stand-off that finally characterizes a containing way of life.

A historicist criticism capable of recognizing the complexities of this kind of permanent contestation of meaning both in the past and in the present cannot and does not, unlike traditional criticism, pretend to be politically neutral. In the words of Dollimore and Sinfield it 'knows that no cultural practice is ever without political significance' and it recognizes that that principle applies to itself. Its design will thus be deliberately interventionist in the name of the here and now. Committed both to the study of 'the implication of literary texts in history' and to 'the transformation of a social order which exploits people on grounds of race, gender and class', it is thereby committed to seeing history as an arena, a site of struggle where, in the name of this commitment, battle must be joined.[8]

3

A Right Bastard

It is time to go back to the beginning of the play. A minor surprise awaits us there; for the truth is that the play does not actually commence with Lear's division of his kingdom, as many critics suppose, but with a few seconds' apparently idle conversation. However, this genuine beginning turns out to be far from irrelevant to the central concerns mentioned in Chapter 1 and indeed confirms their centrality.

Three men walk out on to the stage. The two older men – they are Kent and Gloucester – are talking about King Lear, and Kent's opening remark constitutes the play's first line:

I thought the King had more affected the Duke of Albany than Cornwall.

(I. i. 1)

That apparently odd term 'affected' should now immediately make us prick up our ears. Most footnotes to the text will gloss it, somewhat lamely, as 'loved'. However, that in itself suddenly takes on considerable significance here, for there's no doubt that a sense of evaluation, of weighing and measuring, fully invests the word. In fact, there is every indication that the 'affection' it speaks of will turn out to be entirely congruent with the reduced kind of 'loving' we will encounter when Lear calls for the map. What confronts us then – an account of one duke being 'assessed' in comparison with another – is effectively a preview of what is going to take place between Lear and his daughters in a few seconds' time. In other words, right from the first moments of the play, a wholly debased kind of 'loving' can be seen to operate throughout Lear's court and to inform all of its procedures. Its connection with calculation and with money receives direct confirmation in Gloucester's response to Kent:

> It did always seem so to us; but now, in the division of the kingdom, it appears not which of the Dukes he values most; for equalities are so weigh'd that curiosity in neither can make choice of either's moiety.
>
> (I, i. 3–7)

Here the terms 'division', 'values', 'equalities', 'weigh'd', 'choice', 'moiety' (portion) tell a clear enough story about a kingdom that is about to be parcelled up and shared out, and the spirit of 'loving' or 'affection' in which this is to be done. They prepare us to some degree for the shocks which will follow upon Lear's call for the map, and confirm that it is appropriate to see it as the fulcrum of the play's action. They also establish that in both dimensions of the play's narrative, the story of Lear and the story of Gloucester, the central figures debase the act of loving. Where Lear reduces love to the level of the assessment of the price of land and property, Gloucester reduces love to the level of lust gratified by a whore. In both cases, the values of money mix with and corrupt those of affection in a process of grotesque diminution blithely unnoticed by the perpetrators. In this way, the stories of Gloucester and Lear could be said to intertwine from the beginning of the play, with each offering, in a different key perhaps, a reprise of the concerns of the other.

At this point, Kent appears suddenly to change the subject: indicating the silent figure of Edmund, he asks:

> Is not this your son, my Lord?
>
> (I. i. 8)

Gloucester's reply confirms that the subject has not in fact been changed. The reduced notion of 'love', and its commitment to money, has rarely had a better embodiment than in the tired levity of the ensuing exchange:

> GLOUCESTER. His breeding, Sir, hath been at my charge: I have so often blush'd to acknowledge him, that now I am braz'd to't.
> KENT. I cannot conceive you.
> GLOUCESTER. Sir, this young fellow's mother could; whereupon she

grew round-womb'd, and had, indeed, Sir, a son for her cradle ere she had a husband for her bed. Do you smell a fault?

KENT. I cannot wish the fault undone, the issue of it being so proper.

GLOUCESTER. But I have a son, Sir, by order of law, some year elder than this, who yet is no dearer in my account: though this knave came something saucily to the world before he was sent for, yet was his mother fair; there was good sport at his making, and the whoreson must be acknowledged.

(I. i. 9–24)

Edmund is illegitimate. Worse, his mother was a prostitute and he is a 'whoreson'. To characterize him in conventional terms, so far as the play's early modern audience is concerned, he is the product of lust, not love: of a 'love' reduced to the level of the money involved in the transaction that produced him. Inevitably, he will be tainted by such a background, and the play seems, accordingly, to depict him as the source of unmitigated evil.

As modern readers of the play, of course, our responses to Edmund and the context from which he springs will be quite different. His good looks, for instance (he is a 'proper' young man), to say nothing of the dash and vigour of his subsequent pronouncements and actions, may draw us to him: both Goneril and Regan are certainly drawn. But the Jacobean response to this is slightly more subtle. Evil must be attractive; how else would it succeed? Many of Shakespeare's villains are good-looking and appealing for exactly this reason – Iago in *Othello* is a fine example. That Satan is in some ways the most winsome character in Milton's *Paradise Lost* is certainly no accident.

There are other factors, too. We tend, not unreasonably, to regard illegitimate children with sympathy, and we would certainly not think of imposing on them penalties and deprivations in the manner of previous societies. However, the early modern standard response to illegitimate children was formed by a different set of considerations. First, for a society committed, as we have seen, to kingship as its fundamental form of government, the principle of legitimacy constitutes the very basis of political stability and continuity. It ensures that the right person inherits the supreme position of political power, and of course it becomes an issue whenever succession to the throne is in doubt. Elizabeth herself had been denounced from time to time by her enemies as the illegitimate child of Henry VIII. Second, whenever the transfer of property and money from one generation to another stands as a central mode of financial stability, then the maxim of primogeniture on which it rests owes its validity to the principle of legitimacy. Third, in the absence of any effective means of contraception, and in the presence of virulent and deadly forms of sexually transmitted diseases against which there was no effective defence, sex beyond the confines of marriage – freewheeling, unrestricted sexuality in what used to be the modern pre-AIDS mode – will obviously be judged dangerously disruptive. A socially, politically, and financially destabilizing force, it will seem as potentially explosive a factor as any Gunpowder Plot.

There can be no doubt that Edmund represents just such a force. His self-defining speech at the beginning of Act I, Scene ii (when the play is still only minutes old), offers a highly persuasive justification of unencumbered carnality; of a powerful sexuality confined by no social restrictions. Indeed, Edmund proclaims his allegiance, not to society, nor to 'custom' and its laws, but to the apparently opposing and overriding 'law' of an unrestricted 'nature':

> Thou, Nature, art my goddess; to thy law
> My services are bound. Wherefore should I
> Stand in the plague of custom, and permit
> The curiosity of nations to deprive me,
> For that I am some twelve or fourteen moonshines
> Lag of a brother? Why bastard? Wherefore base?
> When my dimensions are as well compact,
> My mind as generous, and my shape as true
> As honest madam's issue? Why brand they us
> With base? with baseness? bastardy? base, base?
> Who in the lusty stealth of nature take
> More composition and fierce quality
> Than doth, within a dull, stale, tired bed,
> Go to th' creating a whole tribe of fops,
> Got 'tween asleep and wake?

(I. ii. 1–15)

The pounding emphasis of the alliteration (to say nothing of the ribaldry capable of being released by the slightest glance towards the 'tribe of fops' sitting in seats reserved for the high-born on the stage itself) embodies an attractive, convention-shattering energy which is as hard to resist as the scandalous argument it sustains and the abandoned, sarcastic ruthlessness of the plot it then projects:

> Well then,
> Legitimate Edgar, I must have your land:
> Our father's love is to the bastard Edmund
> As to th' legitimate. Fine word, 'legitimate'!
> Well, my legitimate, if this letter speed,
> And my invention thrive, Edmund the base
> Shall top th' legitimate – : I grow, I prosper;
> Now, gods, stand up for bastards!

(I. ii. 15–22)

His brother Edgar's legitimacy is of course finally and decisively desecrated in the pun on 'top' (pronounced in much the same way as 'tup', a verb used to refer to the sexual intercourse of animals) as Edmund presents his triumph in the crudest of sexual metaphors placed in a context of militant male tumescence: 'I grow, I prosper; | Now, gods, stand up for bastards!' Reinforced, no doubt, by appropriately lewd gestures from the actor (and, once more, perhaps, drawing on the presence of the 'fops' sitting on the stage), this offers a moment of potential bonding between actor and audience in which a kind of anarchic fellowship – pitting 'us' against the petty restrictions of 'them' – is hard to resist. Yet even as it takes place, whether as laughter, or applause, or simple sympathy for an 'underdog', the play's structure unerringly complicates and taints it, turning the slightest taste for Edmund's disarming vigour into the very factor that empowers his evil.

Or does it? Is to warm to Edmund here to condone him later? His speech is a good example of the sort of moment in a play where a 'cultural-materialist' account of the text asks a number of questions. There is no doubt that the play requires Edmund to be a villain, perhaps the most appalling villain of the tragedies. Any 'historicist' reading will point to early modern notions of the implications of illegitimacy as a clear signal of this, on the grounds presented above. And it will deal with his undoubted attractiveness in the way that has been suggested, arguing that, to be

21

genuinely effective, evil must also be compelling. His speech, according to this logic, should be the occasion for – if anything – vigorous hissing and booing.

So the moment when, at its conclusion, we can suppose that an audience might almost feel sympathetic towards Edmund – might even laugh with him, applaud his ribald gestures, be persuaded by his rhetoric that illegitimacy has its point – is a powerful and a disturbing one. The actor's capacity, alone on the stage, to manipulate the audience's response with some precision will make the moment crucial. What, then, is our response to be?

The only answer is to reject the possibility of a once-for-all resolution of this potential contradiction, to accept that such undecidable moments are characteristic of all texts, and to take on board the principle that any reading of any text derives its conclusions from the way in which it handles these passages. If our reading of *King Lear* finds its response to Edmund's speech inconclusive, being pulled one way by the apparent intent of the scene and the other way by the potential for performance which the words also contain, then what confronts us is a situation in which to some extent logic (what is said) finds itself undermined by rhetoric (the way in which it is said). In short, the story's clear injunction to us to disapprove of illegitimacy turns out to be drastically at odds with the rhythm, the tone, the gestures, the alliterative and bodily momentum which builds up its over-whelming energy in Edmund's lines.

The result is a fundamental confusion, a moment of genuine contradiction, a point where clear, coherent meaning seems to vanish, and something contradictory, boundary-challenging, impossible to pin down – impossible to 'read' – momentarily erupts. Its newly released energy is both frightening and exciting. No wonder. Edmund, after all, here speaks powerfully, and literally from the centre of the stage, on behalf of those whom his society wishes to silence, and to marginalize. It could be argued that exactly this kind of unresolvable breakdown of logic and co-herence – inevitable whenever the periphery invades the centre – lies at the heart of *King Lear*.

4

Being Reasonable

Not that the play fails also to confront its opposite: reason. Far from it. Indeed, one way to describe Lear's reductive proposal in respect of the measurement of his daughters' love for him would be to call it 'rational'. In a sense, the root of his reductive programme lies here. After all, Lear's is the voice of reason. Every aspect of his monarchy bears what he calls 'the marks of sovereignty, knowledge, and reason' (I. iv. 240). Yet what he proposes to weigh, measure, and evaluate with his reason is something traditionally said to lie beyond its scope – at least beyond the scope of that 'instrumental' kind of reason by whose lights we perform our material operations on the world.[1] Yet this is exactly the basis on which Lear proposes to divide his kingdom:

> Tell me, my daughters,
> (Since now we will divest us both of rule,
> Interest of territory, cares of state)
> Which of you shall we say doth love us most?
> That we our largest bounty may extend
> Where nature doth with merit challenge.

(I. i. 48–53)

The equation this puts forward, that a specific amount of love will be judged to be commensurate with a specific parcel of land, involves precisely a rational – albeit absurd – computation of equalities. And, as we have seen, the play condemns and diagnoses this absurdity unequivocally as reductive. His daughters' fawning replies may bring them their reward –

GONERIL. Sir, I love you more than word can wield the matter;
Dearer than eye-sight, space and liberty;

Beyond what can be valued rich or rare;
No less than life, with grace, health, beauty, honour;
As much as child e'er lov'd, or father found;
A love that makes breath poor and speech unable;
Beyond all manner of so much I love you.

(I. i. 55–61)

REGAN. I am made of that self metal as my sister,
And prize me at her worth. In my true heart
I find she names my very deed of love;
Only she comes too short . . .

(I. i. 69–72)

– but of course in the process they also implicate them in the equation and its demeaning presuppositions. Only Cordelia, with her absolute refusal even to take part in this kind of exercise, manages to remain untainted by it. It is noticeable that her unequivocal response to Lear's invitation –

LEAR.   . . . what can you say to draw
A third more opulent than your sisters? Speak.
CORDELIA. Nothing, my lord.

(I. i. 85–7)

– draws only a furious reiteration of the principle of rational computation from her father:

LEAR. Nothing?
CORDELIA. Nothing.
LEAR. Nothing will come of nothing: speak again.

(I. i. 88–90)

In terms of the equations which dominate and form Lear's reduced, computing world, nothing *can* come of nothing, and Cordelia's efforts to stay within the bounds of what may be measurable and weighable in law in order to please her father –

Good my Lord,
You have begot me, bred me, lov'd me: I

Return those duties back as are right fit,
Obey you, love you, and most honour you.

(I. i. 95–8)

– are not enough. That she cannot resist pointing out Lear's absurd rationality –

Why have my sisters husbands, if they say
They love you all? Happily, when I shall wed,
That lord whose hand must take my plight shall carry
Half my love with him, half my care and duty:
Sure I shall never marry like my sisters,
To love my father all.

(I. i. 99–104)

– merely seals her fate, and she is summarily and cruelly discarded.

Of course, there is nothing 'realistic' in this. No real-life parent, we can presume, would behave in such a manner, and critical agonizing over Lear's 'actual' motives, anxious probings after the 'real' roots of his behaviour, must be judged wasted effort. Effectively, they constitute attempts to turn one form of art into another. The 'emblematic' art of the early modern stage was the inheritor of an ancient European tradition in which the focus and concern of the artist was on 'public' themes: matters of politics, theology, the morality of various forms of governance. This is the art still observable in the carvings and stained-glass windows of European churches, in which moral apothegms and formulae – say that 'Knowledge Triumphs over Ignorance', or that 'Love Conquers Lust' – are presented by means of a picture, a carving, or a woodcut – an *emblem*, that is – depicting, as it might be, St George in the act of slaying the dragon. It is certainly not the 'naturalistic' art of the late nineteenth and early twentieth centuries which interests itself in the psychological structures and workings of individual human beings in specific and life-like settings. That art is concerned with what goes on 'inside' people, with their motives, feelings, and emotional conflicts, and its most potent form is perhaps the novel. But, as we have seen, the great public theatres of the early modern period were far more concerned with what goes on 'outside' characters, in the public arena,

25

and with the 'public' concerns of kingship, politics, and so on. *King Lear* is a play designed for that kind of context. That is, it is the sort of non-naturalistic art, put on in the afternoon, in daylight and in the public gaze, with little attempt at make-up, costume, or 'realistic' sets, and with all its female parts played by male actors, which aimed to engage with 'real' life, not at the private, personal, psychological level, but at the level of the broad, general issues of the common weal and in the mode of public debate.

No better example of 'emblematic' art could be found than the spectacle which the play now proceeds to construct: the turning of the tables upon Lear, so that the reduced, rational 'loving' he has applied to his daughters is eventually focused on himself.

The process begins at the end of Act II. Amongst the rather odd provisions insisted on by Lear when giving up the throne was his retention of 'The name and all th' addition to a king' (I. i. 136). In practice, it transpires that this means not only that he will keep his title, but that he intends also to keep a retinue of one hundred knights as an important sign of his social and political standing. Moreover, his daughters will be required in turns to provide sustenance and accommodation for him and his men as they travel about the country;

> Ourself, by monthly course,
> With reservation of an hundred knights
> By you to be sustain'd, shall our abode
> Make with you by due turn.

(I. i. 132–5)

By any standards, this could be said to constitute an attempt to have your cake and eat it, and Lear's tyrannical insistence on his rights almost immediately gives rise to complaint. However, the significance of the arrangement lies in its capacity to make a larger point on a level quite beyond that of 'character'.

By the end of Act I Goneril is already complaining to Lear about the behaviour of his knights:

> Men so disorder'd, so debosh'd, and bold,
> That this our court, infected with their manners,
> Shows like a riotous inn: epicurism and lust

> Makes it more like a tavern or a brothel
> Than a grac'd palace.

(I. iv. 250–4)

When she asks him to 'disquantity your train' (I. iv. 257) – to cut the numbers down – Lear's response is predictable:

> Darkness and devils!
> Saddle my horses; call my train together.
> Degenerate bastard! I'll not trouble thee:
> Yet have I left a daughter.

(I. iv. 260–3)

Yet when, in Act II, Scene iv, Lear arrives at Regan's palace, he discovers that his servant Kent has been placed in the stocks, and that Regan (alerted by a letter from her sister) is rather less than sympathetic:

> LEAR.   . . . Beloved Regan,
>   Thy sister's naught: O Regan! she hath tied
>   Sharp-tooth'd unkindness, like a vulture, here.
>
>   .   .   .   .
>
> REGAN. I cannot think my sister in the least
>   Would fail her obligation. If, Sir, perchance
>   She have restrain'd the riots of your followers,
>   'Tis on such ground, and to such wholesome end,
>   As clears her from all blame.
>
>   .   .   .   .
>
>   O, Sir, you are old;
>   Nature in you stands on the very verge
>   Of her confine: you should be rul'd and led
>   By some discretion that discerns your state
>   Better than you yourself. Therefore I pray you
>   That to our sister you do make return;
>   Say you have wrong'd her.

(II. iv. 134–53)

Moments later, Goneril enters, and Lear confronts both his daughters. As he turns with mounting fury and bewilderment from one to the other, the issues of how much each of them loves him, and the number of knights each will allow him to retain, gradually become intertwined. A disturbing project begins to unfurl:

REGAN. I pray you, father, being weak, seem so.
  If, till the expiration of your month,
  You will return and sojourn with my sister,
  Dismissing half your train, come then to me:

  . . . .

LEAR. Return to her? and fifty men dismiss'd?
  No, rather I abjure all roofs, and choose
  To wage against the enmity o' th' air;
  To be a comrade with the wolf and owl,
  Necessity's sharp pinch! Return with her!
  Why, the hot-blooded France, that dowerless took
  Our youngest born, I could as well be brought
  To knee his throne, and, squire-like, pension beg
  To keep base life afoot. Return with her!
  Persuade me rather to be slave and sumpter
  To this detested groom. [*Pointing at Oswald.*]
GONERIL.   At your choice, Sir.
LEAR. I prithee daughter, do not make me mad;
  I will not trouble thee, my child; farewell.
  We'll no more meet, no more see one another;

  . . . .

  I can be patient, I can stay with Regan,
  I and my hundred knights.
REGAN.   Not altogether so;
  I look'd not for you yet, nor am provided
  For your fit welcome. Give ear, Sir, to my sister;
  For those that mingle reason with your passion
  Must be content to think you old, and so –
  But she knows what she does.
LEAR.   Is this well spoken?
REGAN. I dare avouch it, Sir: what! fifty followers
  Is it not well? What should you need of more?
  Yea, or so many . . .

  . . . .

       . . . If you will come to me,
  For now I spy a danger, I entreat you
  To bring but five-and-twenty; to no more
  Will I give place or notice.

(II. iv. 203–51)

In the face of such a programme Lear begins gradually – albeit dimly – to perceive that this proposed measurement of 'giving' might, in the event, prove inappropriate:

> LEAR. I gave you all—
> REGAN.　　　　　And in good time you gave it.
> LEAR. Made you my guardians, my depositaries,
> 　But kept a reservation to be follow'd
> 　With such a number. What! must I come to you
> 　With five and twenty? Regan, said you so?
> REGAN. And speak't again, my Lord; no more with me.
> LEAR. Those wicked creatures yet do look well-favour'd
> 　When others are more wicked; not being the worst
> 　Stands in some rank of praise.

(II. iv. 252–60)

– and then, turning to Goneril, he utters again, this time quite openly, the pitiful equation that confirms the reduced nature of that measuring, computing 'loving' of which he was himself first guilty:

> 　　　　　　　　　I'll go with thee:
> Thy fifty yet doth double five-and-twenty,
> And thou art twice her love.

(II. iv. 260–2)

It is an astonishing moment. Loving and measuring coincide here, in exactly the mode that Lear had initially cast them. The tables are precisely turned upon the perpetrator of this tragedy and its principles are now remorselessly applied to himself. His daughters then proceed relentlessly to ram home its full reductive import:

> GONERIL.　　　　　　Hear me, my Lord.
> What need you five-and-twenty, ten, or five,
> To follow in a house where twice so many
> Have a command to tend you?

(II. iv. 262–5)

It is left to Regan to perform the *coup de grace*:

> What need one?
>
> (II. iv. 265)

The withering, reductive nature of instrumental, weighing, measuring, assessing reason that Lear has unleashed upon the world could scarcely be more starkly revealed. Its effect is immediate and shattering. Lear erupts violently, rounding on his daughters and in the process rounding upon the sort of reasoning that they – and he – have embodied:

> O! reason not the need; out basest beggars
> Are in the poorest thing superfluous:
> Allow not nature more than nature needs,
> Man's life is cheap as beast's.
>
> (II. iv. 266–9)

His point, that the full dimensions of human 'need' are literally immeasurable and cannot be weighed and assessed in modes appropriate to those of an instrumental reason, comments sharply on his own previous behaviour. With the judgement that to treat human beings so is to treat them as cattle, he condemns himself. If 'need' is measured solely in the quantitative terms that have been applied to Lear's own retinue of knights, terms that he applied earlier to the love of his own daughters, then beggars might even be said to have more than they 'need'. But the harsh lesson Lear is learning is that true human needs are not capable of assessment in that way. He tries vainly to make the point to Regan –

> Thou art a lady;
> If only to go warm were gorgeous,
> Why, nature needs not what thou gorgeous wear'st,
> Which scarcely keeps thee warm. But, for true need, –
> You Heavens, give me that patience, patience I need! –
> You see me here, you Gods, a poor old man . . .
>
> (II. iv. 269–74)

– but the insight dissolves into rage and blustering:

> No, you unnatural hags,
> I will have such revenges on you both
> That all the world shall – I will do such things,
> What they are, yet I know not, but they shall be
> The terrors of the earth.

> (II. iv. 280–4)

In all the sound and fury, it is Lear's own crime that surfaces with pointed and powerful irony here, at what is perhaps another pivotal point of the play's action. Condemned out of his own mouth, Lear ultimately finds himself pushed over a brink on which he has teetered from the beginning. And as that happens, a larger irony stands suddenly revealed:

> You think I'll weep;
> No, I'll not weep:
> I have full cause of weeping, [*Storm heard at a
> distance*] but this heart
> Shall break into a hundred thousand flaws
> Or ere I'll weep. O Fool! I shall go mad.

> (II. iv. 284–8)

The great wielder and advocate of reason has begun to lose his own hold on precisely that faculty.

REGAN. I am made of that self metal as my sister,
And prize me at her worth.

(I. i. 69-70)

I

Angus McBean

LEAR. Nothing will come of nothing: speak again.

(I. i. 89-90)

II

LEAR. Dost thou call me fool, boy!

(I. iv. 154)

III

LEAR. Blow, winds, and crack your cheeks! rage! blow!

(III. ii. 1)

IV

EDGAR. Come on, sir; here's the place: stand still. How fearful
   And dizzy 'tis to cast one's eyes so low!

(IV. vi. 11-12)

V

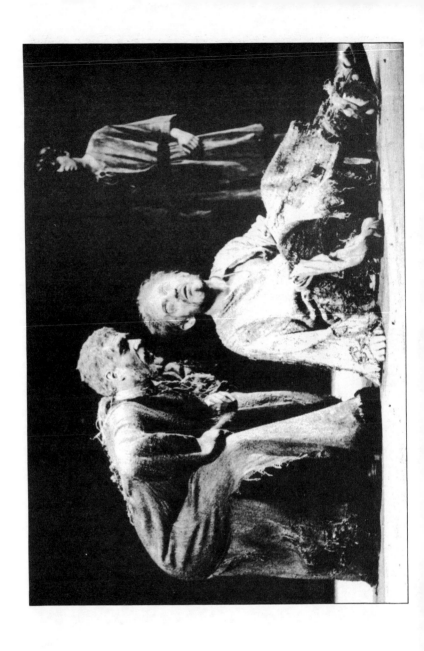

LEAR. What! art mad? A man may see how this world goes with no
eyes.

(IV. vi. 150-151)

Angus McBean

CORDELIA.   Was this a face
    To be oppos'd against the warring winds?

(IV. vii. 31-2)

VII

5

Reason and Madness: Male and Female

'What need one?' Regan's question raises exactly the dimension of existence – human need – with which Lear's reason has proved unable to cope. Yet simply to say that he goes mad at this point in the play is perhaps to lessen the impact of what happens. Lear certainly reaches and goes beyond the limit of his rational faculty. However, the effect of that is to reveal how limited a notion of that faculty has hitherto engaged him. To have some sense of what an alternative might be, we will have to move back once more towards the beginning of the play.

When Cordelia refuses even to take part in Lear's division of the kingdom, rejecting the very grounds on which his equation of love and land rests, she instigates, by that act, an opposite 'pole' from the one to which her sisters, Lear, and most of his court are apparently committed. If we characterize the mode which Goneril, Regan, and Lear exemplify as 'rational', then Cordelia, and the sort of thinking she embodies, seem to qualify as 'irrational'.

But there is a better concept, which perhaps avoids the modern connotations of that word. It would have been familiar to Shakespeare's audience in terms of an expanded sense of the human reason which allowed that its merely instrumental capacities were limited by the 'fallen', earth-bound nature of humanity. Nevertheless, a residue of non-earth-bound, non-instrumental reason remained available to human beings. This 'superior' reason had access to exactly those regions from which the 'lower' reason was debarred, and its use linked humankind to God. Its mode was instantaneous, non-laboured, involving something like the process we now label 'intuitive'. But, of course, seen from the point of view of the 'lower' reason, it often appeared as a kind of 'madness'.

Such a concept obviously provides the basis for the paradoxical idea of a 'perceptive' madness, or foolishness, in which the apparently irrational proves capable of genuine 'insight' whilst the rational remains lamely imperceptive, or blind. Analogues of this major paradox run throughout Shakespeare's plays. Lovers, possessed, like the mad, of 'intuitive' insight, rather than rational judgement, are able to 'see' more clearly than ordinary folk, even though, like Cupid, they may seem blind. Indeed, the blind (like ancient poets) often turn out to be 'seers', the mad (like ancient prophets) frequently turn out to be sagacious, fools can show themselves to be genuinely 'wise'. As Theseus puts it in *A Midsummer Night's Dream*:

> Lovers and madmen have such seething brains,
> Such shaping fantasies, that apprehend
> More than cool reason ever comprehends.

> (V. i. 4–6)

In *King Lear*, a play in which madness and blindness play such central roles, the concept of a superior form of reasoning is firmly rooted in the character of Cordelia from the beginning, and her future husband, France, denies Lear's 'rational' assessment of her guilt in precisely those terms:

> which to believe of her,
> Must be a faith that reason without miracle
> Should never plant in me.

> (I. i. 221–3)

Lear's response to Cordelia's non-rational rejection of an assessing process that would have made her rich is to brand his daughter 'foolish' in the extreme. Of course, by that token, he also links her with the 'official' representative of foolishness in the play. Indeed, at the thematic level, Cordelia and the Fool can be said to become almost interchangeable. For, whilst Cordelia is banished from Lear's sight, the Fool remains, serving to a large extent as the representative of the pole opposed to reason and, in Cordelia's absence, as its most effective voice. The fact that Cordelia and the Fool never appear on the stage together – added to the fact that all female parts on the early modern stage were in any case played by males – suggests that their linking could easily be reinforced if the part were 'doubled' – that is, if Cordelia and the Fool were seen, transparently, to be played by the same male actor.

Be that as it may, the Fool nevertheless makes certain that the point of view for which Cordelia stands in the story is maintained when she is off-stage. As a result, once Cordelia is banished, the Fool's presence in Lear's company becomes pervasive. Rising above the level of direct influence on the plot, he begins to function almost as a chorus to the action, commenting sometimes obliquely, sometimes almost directly, on its developments in terms of an 'intuitive' non-rationality which none the less quite starkly points out the reality and the consequences of Lear's actions:

> FOOL. . . . Nuncle, give me an egg, and I'll give thee two crowns.
> LEAR. What two crowns shall they be?
> FOOL. Why, after I have cut the egg i' th' middle and eat up the meat, the two crowns of the egg. When thou clovest thy crown i' th' middle, and gav'st away both parts, thou bor'st thine ass on thy back o'er the dirt: thou hadst little wit in thy bald crown when thou gav'st thy golden one away.
>
> (I. iv. 162–71)

Time and again, the Fool presents Lear with the grotesque overriding paradox that results from his actions. He even displays it physically, on the stage:

> That lord that counsell'd thee
> To give away thy land,
> Come place him here by me,
> Do thou for him stand:
> The sweet and bitter fool
> Will presently appear;
> The one in motley here,
> The other found out there.
>
> (I. iv. 146–53)

When the king shows himself to be a fool, then the Fool has a good claim to be a king. The two 'fools' – the one in motley who sees the truth, the other, wearing the crown, who is blind to it – confront each other here, and the point is materially and visually made. Lear, although rational, is foolish. The fool, non-rational, is wise. It is thus not inappropriate that Lear's angry 'Dost thou call me fool, boy?' meets with the Fool's riposte 'All thy other titles thou hast given away; that thou wast born with', drawing in the process Kent's perceptive comment 'This is not altogether Fool, my Lord' (I. iv. 154–7).

At other times, the Fool will speak of values which exist above the rational level on which they can be 'known' or 'shown', and which outstrip the computation of Lear's 'Nothing will come of nothing' precisely because of that:

> Mark it, Nuncle:
>> Have more than thou showest,
>> Speak less than thou knowest,
>
>> .   .   .   .
>
>> And thou shalt have more
>> Than two tens to a score.
>
> (I. iv. 123–33)

In fact, the Fool's mockery of Lear's arrogant mathematics is virtually overt, pointing directly to the crime that Lear has committed in equating the value of land with that of love:

> FOOL. . . . Can you make no use of nothing, Nuncle?
> LEAR. Why no, boy; nothing can be made out of nothing.
> FOOL [to Kent]. Prithee, tell him, so much the rent of his land comes to: he will not believe a Fool.
>
> (I. iv. 136–41)

'He will not believe a Fool' could be Lear's motto. It contains the essence of his tragedy because it refers both to the Fool himself, and to Cordelia. Perhaps Lear recognizes their unity right at the end of the play. By then completely irrational, he enters with the dead Cordelia in his arms and, showing her body to the audience, announces that 'my poor fool is hang'd'! (V. iii. 305).

To such a reading of the roles of Cordelia and the Fool, we might now usefully add a further dimension. It has to do with matters of sex and gender and the issues at stake are important enough to make it worth while sketching out some of their potentially salient features and noting ways in which these might be developed. A 'gendered' reading of *King Lear* will not necessarily limit itself to a concern with the function of women in the play. Its first broad principle will be that the roles inherited by both males and females in society are not 'naturally' given, or characterized by any 'essential' features inherited by either group. There is nothing in nature that requires this range of social activity and behaviour to be assigned to women and that to men, or which says that women must behave in this particular way, and men in that. A 'gendered' reading of the play will rather seek to discover how the roles which seem 'natural' to each gender are constructed, what functions they perform, and what sort of society they apparently derive from and in turn reinforce. It will want to do so partly on the grounds that knowledge of how such matters were ordered in the early modern period are obviously of serious consequence to its inheritors.

If, then, we accept Coppelia Kahn's view that Shakespeare 'explores the unconscious attitudes behind cultural definitions of manliness and womanliness and behind the mores and institutions shaped by them', it will obviously be important to register that, right at the beginning of *King Lear*, 'traditional' roles seem unquestioningly to be assigned to females in respect of the functions of wife, daughter, and lover.[1] Lear's approach to his daughters quite clearly enacts the primary features of a patriarchal society. Family relations are firmly established, hierarchical and unchangeable, with authority securely in place at the top. The father's word, like the king's, may be questioned or disobeyed only at extreme peril.

In the case of Gloucester and his offspring Edmund, the standard distinction between wife and lover is also maintained. The progeny resulting from union with a wife is 'legitimate', that from union with a woman outside marriage is 'illegitimate', even though the latter – by implied contrast with the former – was the occasion of 'great sport'. The wives of Gloucester and Lear, the mothers, that is, of Edgar on the one hand and Goneril, Regan, and Cordelia on the other, to say nothing of the mother of Edmund, are all mentioned in the play. However, despite the fact that both the play's stories turn on the relationship between parents and their children, these women do not appear on the stage. Not only does the crucially nurturing mother-child relationship turn out to be absent, but – by virtue of the fact that mothers are referred to – their shadowy, insubstantial presence/absence on the play's periphery begins to acquire its own significance. Coppelia Kahn has pointed out that such a situation serves to stress that, in this society, 'the only source of love, power and authority is the father – an awesome, demanding presence', and Mary Beth Rose speaks of a certain Elizabethan sense that in a desirable adult society the 'best mother is an absent or dead mother'.[2]

By contrast, men emerge from this analysis as supremely rational, dominant beings, embodiments of physical 'presence' and undoubtedly in charge of their destiny and of their women. In the case of Edmund, whose assertive masculinity, as we have seen, is the subject of intense and memorable focus, Gloucester's lust seems to have had momentous results cognate with Lear's 'rational' division of the kingdom, to a degree that perhaps warrants the labelling of Lear's 'marks of sovereignty, knowledge, and reason' as 'male'.

What the play chronicles, of course, is a fundamental challenge to that male reason, a condemnation of its parameters as narrow and constricted, and of its processes as divisive and reductive. It is significant that such a challenge comes precisely from the female Cordelia, or from her surrogate voice, that of the Fool. It is also significant that it comes in the form of the 'super-rational', whose mode can be termed 'intuitive'.

Whether or not the play could be said coherently to depict and endorse the emergence of a 'woman's reason' – still faintly recognizable to us, perhaps, in its reduced, popular guise as 'intuition' – will depend on the degree to which the strategies of this sort of reading are pursued.[3] It does perhaps tend to construct and promote an all-too-recognizable 'Shakespeare' figure, benign culture-hero and prescient author, a 'new man' before his time, for whom the plays are merely mouthpieces for the dissemination of his wholly admirable late-twentieth-century liberal sentiments. It ignores the extent to which any text responds to and is part of the context which surrounds it. Kathleen McLuskie, arguing that *King Lear* exhibits a specific notion of women characteristic of the early modern period, rightly warns us that 'Shakespeare's plays are not primarily explorations of "the real nature of women" or even "the hidden feelings of the human heart". They were the products of an entertainment industry which, as far as we know, had no women shareholders, actors, writers, or stage hands.'[4]

There are undoubtedly powerful moments of apparent misogyny in the play, matching the inherent prejudices of that set-up, in which women will find themselves castigated as the springs of corruption in powerful and appallingly specific terms. Lear's recollection, in his madness, of his daughters' perfidy produces this outburst:

> Let copulation thrive; for Gloucester's bastard son
> Was kinder to his father than my daughters
> Got 'tween the lawful sheets. To't, Luxury, pell-mell!
> For I lack soldiers. Behold yond simp'ring dame,
> Whose face between her forks presages snow;
> That minces virtue, and does shake the head
> To hear of pleasure's name;
> The fitchew nor the soiled horse goes to't
> With a more riotous appetite.
> Down from the waist they are Centaurs,
> Though women all above:
> But to the girdle do the Gods inherit,
> Beneath is all the fiend's: there's hell, there's darkness,
> There is the sulphurous pit – burning, scalding,
> Stench, consumption; fie, fie, fie! pah, pah!

(IV. vi. 117–31)

However, the play is also at some pains to explore the notion that social manners conceal an inner, moral corruption. A metaphor of fine clothing or moral posturing which hides a depraved reality is no less appropriate to that theme, so that these sentiments could reasonably be said to be also part of a different and recurring motif. The following words of Lear occur within seconds of the above and are clearly more than sympathetic to the plight of some women, and indeed that of humanity at large:

> Thou rascal beadle, hold thy bloody hand!
> Why dost thou lash that whore? Strip thine own back;
> Thou hotly lusts to use her in that kind
> For which thou whipp'st her. The usurer hangs the cozener.
> Thorough tatter'd clothes small vices do appear;
> Robes and furr'd gowns hide all. Plate sin with gold,

And the strong lance of justice hurtless breaks;
Arm it in rags, a pygmy's straw does pierce it.
None does offend, none, I say, none . . .

(IV. vi. 162–70)

There are equally powerful moments in the play when the text yields itself quite readily to a specific notion of the female, which Lear longs to embrace. His mad speech, for example, heard moments after the rational assessment of his retinue of knights by his daughters –

Blow, winds, and crack your cheeks! rage! blow!
You cataracts and hurricanoes, spout
Till you have drench'd our steeples, drown'd the cocks!
You sulph'rous and thought-executing fires,
Vaunt-couriers of oak-cleaving thunderbolts,
Singe my white head! And thou, all-shaking thunder,
Strike flat the thick rotundity o' th' world!
Crack Nature's moulds, all germens spill at once
That makes ingrateful man!

(III. ii. 1–9)

– gestures towards gigantic birth-pangs at the same time as it speaks of universal destruction. It is as if his abandonment of reason genuinely involves the abandonment of a tough and heartless maleness. In this motherless play, Lear's incipient madness even detects the malady *hysterica passio* – significantly termed the 'mother' – in his own body (II. iv. 56–8). The sight of Edgar on the Heath intensifies the process of purgation and results in the stripping-away of the harsh 'manliness' which reason has urged upon its proponents here, to reveal a nakedness stark and shockingly vulnerable:

Is man no more than this? Consider him well. Thou ow'st the worm no silk, the beast no hide, the sheep no wool, the cat no perfume.

(III. iv. 105–8)

Lear's stripping-away of his own clothes involves a divestment of the same manly falsity:

Ha! here's three on's are sophisticated; thou are the thing itself;

39

unaccommodated man is no more but such a poor, bare, forked animal
as thou art. Off, off, you lendings! Come; unbutton here.

(III. iv. 108–12)

Stripped of a 'rational' gender role that has misled and betrayed
him, the new-born 'thing itself; unaccommodated man' is thus
enabled, through the abandonment of reason, to make contact
with a more genuine notion of maleness in terms of the 'poor,
bare, forked animal' that lies beneath. Perhaps this makes possible
a reconciliation with a feminine dimension that has hitherto been
fiercely excluded. Maybe a true 'man' has, in the end, to slough
off a limited notion of reason and commit himself to a genuinely
'foolish' pattern of existence – the sort of life Lear proposes for
himself and Cordelia when they are reunited;

> Come let's away to prison;
> We two alone will sing like birds i' th' cage:
> When thou dost ask me blessing, I'll kneel down,
> And ask of thee forgiveness: so we'll live,
> And pray, and sing, and tell old tales, and laugh
> At gilded butterflies, and hear poor rogues
> Talk of court news; and we'll talk with them too,
> Who loses and who wins; who's in, who's out;
> And take upon's the mystery of things,
> As if we were God's spies . . .

(V. iii. 8–17)

There can be no question that, as part of its concern with large
public matters, *King Lear* registers almost seismographically an
early modern tension between genders as a dimension of, and
thus potentially an apt metaphor for, different ways of conceiving
or perceiving the world. To the extent that the play is critical of
an instrumental reason, it can be said to be critical of the sort of
maleness whose instrument that reason is.

6

Masterless Men

Whether or not the notions of maleness and of femaleness at work in the play should be seen as dominant aspects of its impact depends on the position from which the critic speaks and the project to which he or she is finally committed. To say that perhaps sounds odd; yet it is to say nothing more than that the play is a text. However, no text is a transparent window, giving immediate access to a single, coherent meaning somehow lying 'within' itself. Texts are nothing if not inherently plural structures, always open to different readings. And in our society, Shakespearian texts enjoy a special status which turns them into extremely sensitive areas, arenas almost, across which competing ideological forces, in the form of different readings, struggle for the upper hand. The prize is a considerable one; for whoever finally 'owns' Shakespeare could be said to have a good deal of influence on the way in which English speakers the world over tend to perceive 'the way things are'.

To focus on the issue of gender in *King Lear* is perhaps to bring to the centre of the stage something which another reading – not the play 'itself', for there is no 'play itself', only our different readings of it – would place at the periphery. The justification for engaging in such a reading must be that it apparently accords with our current judgement as to what is important in the life of our own culture. That sense of importance increases if we can discern the germ of it at work right at the beginning of the modern period, in the early seventeenth century. It helps us to trace the evolving history of our own culture, and to understand the reasons for its present shape, preoccupations, and presuppositions.

But none of this necessarily means that we are seeing the play as its first audiences saw it and we should be careful to question that illusion. After all, the notions embodied in the very terms

'Elizabethan', 'Jacobean', and 'early modern' are our own. We invent 'the Elizabethans' to some degree, as extensions of our selves: since the past is literally unreachable, we can hardly do otherwise. And we should never forget that one of the most central of our inventions is that all-knowing, all-wise Bardic figure for whom we have constructed the term 'Shakespeare'. That one of his major plays should turn out to focus on a number of our own major concerns is thus hardly surprising. But it is not disabling either, since – and this may at least be an aspect of what 'Shakespeare' is 'for' – it serves to establish and confirm what those concerns genuinely are.

It would be difficult to resist another of these which now seems urgently to manœuvre itself into the foreground. To follow the journey of Lear, Kent, and the Fool across the storm-blasted heath in Acts III and IV is to accompany them into the depths of madness. It is also to witness a number of important encounters. As we have already seen, the first one, with madness, and with the storm ('this tempest in my mind' (III. iv. 12)) that mimics it, seems almost to 'feminize' Lear, to prise open the harsh carapace of rational 'manliness' that had hitherto covered and protected him. His ravings amid the thunder and the lightning still refer to recent events, but they begin to hint at a quite different creature who might emerge from them:

> I tax you not, you elements, with unkindness;
> I never gave you kingdom, call'd you children,
> You owe me no subscription: then let fall
> Your horrible pleasure; here I stand, your slave,
> A poor, infirm, weak, and despis'd old man.

(III. ii. 16–20)

Meeting Kent, this Lear now reveals his dawning awareness – thanks to 'this dreadful pudder o'er our heads' (III. ii. 50) – of the massive extent of the social injustice which his rule has masked:

> Tremble, thou wretch,
> That hast within thee undivulged crimes,
> Unwhipp'd of justice; hide thee, thou bloody hand,
> Thou perjur'd, and thou simular of virtue
> That art incestuous . . .

(III. ii. 51–5)

Finding – he whose 'needs' have been so recently and remorselessly scanned by his daughter – that

> The art of our necessities is strange,
> And can make vile things precious.

(III. ii. 70–1)

he moves to take shelter in a hovel. His situation – desperate,
mad, entirely bereft of the pomp and ceremony with which he
began the play – brings home the enormity of his shortcomings
as a king.

> Poor naked wretches, whereso'er you are,
> That bide the pelting of this pitiless storm,
> How shall your houseless heads and unfed sides,
> Your loop'd and window'd raggedness, defend you
> From seasons such as these? O! I have ta'en
> Too little care of this. Take physic, Pomp;
> Expose thyself to feel what wretches feel,
> That thou mayst shake the superflux to them,
> And show the Heavens more just.

(III. iv. 28–36)

Lear's acknowledgement of the poor and the homeless here, his
admission of his own negligence in the matter, is an important
example of the sort of 'insight' his madness brings, and it
constitutes a significant step on any road to redemption that he
might subsequently take. But to a modern critic it also generates
a moment of intense irony whose implications start to suffuse the
play. The Fool's immediate and horrified discovery that some sort
of 'spirit' seems to be inhabiting the hovel, and the revelation that
this is none other than Gloucester's estranged legitimate son
Edgar, disguised as the madman Poor Tom, create a situation
whose implications are explosive. Not only do the play's two
stories now begin to coincide, but some of their central themes
come to the fore in the tableaux that result.

Edgar is careful to act out the part of Poor Tom in language as
evidently devoid of reason as anything said by Lear –

> Bless thy five wits! Tom's a-cold. O! do de, do de, do de. Bless thee
> from whirlwinds, star-blasting, and taking! Do Poor Tom some charity,

whom the foul fiend vexes. There could I have him now, and there, and there again, and there.

(III. iv. 58–62)

– and Gloucester's later arrival on the scene (III. iv. 116) forces Edgar to complicate this impenetrability even further in order to avoid recognition:

The Prince of Darkness is a gentleman; Modo he's called, and Mahu.

(III. iv. 147–8)

Lear in his madness fails to recognize either Edgar or Gloucester, and his efforts to establish common ground build up a powerful poignancy:

What! has his daughters brought him to this pass?
Couldst thou save nothing? Would'st thou give 'em all?

(III. iv. 63–4)

Here, he who was undoubtedly the highest in the land confronts someone who represents the lowest point on the social scale. That Lear insists they have something in common is certainly significant on a moral level. He has betrayed an elemental humanity in himself and his subjects and that is what now confronts and accuses him in the figure of Poor Tom. As a result, Lear seems prepared to question the validity of the whole social hierarchy:

FOOL. Prithee, Nuncle, tell me whether a madman be a gentleman or a yeoman?
LEAR. A King, a King!

(III. vi. 9–11)

In the mock-trial of Goneril and Regan that Lear then imagines (III. vi. 20 ff.), Poor Tom is promoted to the rank of 'robed man of justice' (III. vi. 37), with the Fool as his colleague, his 'yokefellow of equity' (III. vi. 38). Lear's piteous complaints:

. . . let them anatomize Regan, see what breeds about her heart. Is there any cause in nature that make these hard hearts?

(III. vi. 77–9)

move them to tears. And yet there is a further dimension. Poor Tom would surely have been recognized by the audience as a representation of a well-known bugbear from real life, and at the time the source of periodic bouts of moral panic; one of that band of half-starved, half-crazed figures who were beginning in increasing numbers to gather on the periphery of communities in the early modern period. Haunting the outskirts of villages and the suburbs of towns, wandering across inhospitable open places, unhoused, ungoverned, unrestrained, they were known as 'masterless men' – a title which gives a clue as to some of the social presuppositions defining their situation.[1]

One of its causes was a reorganization of methods of working the land: it was known as 'enclosure'. In essence, enclosure involved the amalgamation of the ancient medieval strips, farmed by individual tenants, into much larger units, farmed more profitably by fewer people. To 'enclose' land was to consolidate its resources in a way designed to make it what we term 'cost-effective'. In addition, so contemporary landowners argued, it helped to flush out the 'multiplicity of beggars' known to congregate on unenclosed land. It also dispossessed a large number of tenant farmers, who accordingly became, to use a modern term, 'redundant'.

The historian Christopher Hill had pointed out that a major consequence of the enclosure movement was to force its victims into 'dependence on wage labour': that is, it forced them into what we would call 'jobs' and into a relationship between work and life dominated by the concept of 'employment' and its related 'wage'. We can recognize in that something quite new and quite different from an older way of thinking which did not divide 'work' from a whole complex involvement with an entire way of life. One did not work at a job and then, as it were, live one's life as a separate entity. One did what had to be done in order to live: 'work' and 'life' were inextricably mingled. To create a separate compartment in experience called 'employment' – involving a job for which one is paid – is also to create its opposite: the absence of a job and the absence of pay. In short, although the 'masterless men' represented a new phenomenon for the early modern period, it is one that a twentieth-century audience, as inheritors of so many of that period's innovations, will recognize immediately: unemployment.

At these climactic moments in the play, then, a representative of the 'unemployed' periphery of the society confronts, and makes common cause with the king who is at its centre. Lear goes so far as to pronounce Poor Tom a 'Noble philosopher' (III. iv. 176) and proposes to consult him about important matters. But there is a deeper irony even than that. For by now, the king, too, is unemployed.

7

Roles and Goals

To suggest that *King Lear* is a play which centres on unemployment may seem odd. But it will appear less so once we allow that concept to expand to its fullest stretch in respect of a society which has become fundamentally unhinged. When the 'normal' relationship of human beings to one another and to the world at large begins to fall apart, it is as if the roles which individuals have inherited from generation to generation suddenly cease to be available, as if the costumes in which these have been played no longer fit, and as if the lines that the actors have been given to speak no longer have any meaning.

The theatrical metaphors drawn on here offer a particularly effective purchase on the early modern period. A society in which social functions are inherited and passed from generation to generation is profoundly different from the one we inhabit. If that society is also pre-literate, committed to the sound of the voice and the presence of the body as its primary means of communication, those social functions may even end by being imprinted on the tongue, through the very names by which its members are recognized and known. To be a butcher, a wheelwright, a carter, a smith in such a culture is to inherit a *role*: one whose very name, Butcher, Wheelwright, Carter, Smith, becomes an important part of the linking – or articulation – on which a sense of social identity and cohesion depends. It is no surprise to discover that, in such role-dominated societies, the art of drama and indeed the whole business of 'playing' a part held a central place, that all the world might well, and with conviction, be said to be a stage, or that a theatre could in all seriousness be called 'The Globe'.

The social and economic changes experienced by early modern Britain effectively involved the destruction of a society of that sort, and its replacement by another whose quite different mode is none the less immediately recognizable to us. Marshall McLuhan has described this change in terms of major disruption. Out of it comes the modern world we know. Viewed from four hundred years on, we can say that those who experienced that disruption confronted and took part in a cataclysmic change involving what McLuhan terms 'a process of stripping and denudation' in which they moved from an oral, pre-industrial, and fundamentally medieval way of life to a literate, industrialized, and fundamentally modern mode of existence.[1] In so far as that new way of life refused the inhibition of inherited functions and structures and, by contrast, stressed individualism, 'getting on', and linear and progressive career-building as the central opportunities it offered, it produced a society committed to the abandonment of 'roles' in favour of the achievement of 'goals'. Being named 'Baker' no longer meant that that was the part you inevitably had to play.

If *King Lear* is seen as a play which to some extent records the initial upheavals of such a gigantic change, then its chronicle of lost certainties, wrecked inheritances, ruined and no-longer-playable roles, its picture of a whole world collapsing in the face of the thrusting individual pursuit of goals by such as Edmund and Goneril and Regan, can be said to construct an extended and apt metaphor of loss, failed connections, misdirected energies, for which some sense of catastrophic 'unemployment' is an acceptable shorthand. On a gigantic and horrific scale, unemployment in that larger sense runs its jagged, dislocating course through this society, undermining everybody from pauper to monarch, like a major earthquake.

Thus, when Lear – mad, ragged, 'cut to th' brains' (IV. vi. 195) – meets Gloucester – blind, suicidal, condemned to 'smell | His way to Dover' (III. vii. 92–3) – the play's crucial themes coalesce in the 'unemployed' displacement both have experienced. Gloucester's is almost literal. With his eyes plucked out at the orders of the vengeful Goneril, Regan, and Edmund, he is fundamentally disorientated, able to see only 'feelingly' (IV. vi. 150), yet forced to rely on Edgar's oddly graphic 'perspectival' description of the view from the cliff from which he hopes to hurl himself:

Come on, sir; here's the place: stand still. How fearful
And dizzy 'tis to cast one's eyes so low!
The crows and choughs that wing the midway air
Show scarce so gross as beetles; half way down
Hangs one that gathers sampire, dreadful trade!
Methinks he seems no bigger than his head.
The fishermen that walk upon the beach
Appear like mice, and yond tall anchoring bark
Diminish'd to her cock, her cock a buoy
Almost too small for sight.

(IV. vi. 11–20)

Renouncing the world, he hurls himself from this imagined height, creating a situation on the stage in which his own disorientation momentarily infects the audience. Of course we can see that this is no 'real' cliff, yet we are unsure at which level of 'reality' the play is currently operating. The mound from which Gloucester jumps – or some other such stage device – would have had in any case to serve as a cliff on the stage if his fall were to count as 'real' in the play's terms. The dizzying perspective and apparent accuracy of Edgar's previous description deliberately confuses us and, for a few seconds after the event, we are uncertain whether Gloucester is supposed genuinely to have fallen from the cliff or not. Rarely has an atmosphere of diffused, dislocating 'unemployment' been so startlingly mimicked. Rarely has the early modern theatre's capacity symbolically to connect with its audience's broad experience, and then suddenly and intensely to crystallize it, been so powerfully demonstrated.

Unable to 'Look up a-height' (IV. vi. 58) and to enter the perspective that Edgar paints, unable to 'see' whether he is dead or alive, half-convinced by Edgar that his preservation is a 'miracle', Gloucester's detachment from the physical world seems almost to purge him of those material impulses which had resulted in the birth of Edmund. He resolves that

henceforth I'll bear
Affliction till it do cry out itself
'Enough, enough', and die.

(IV. vi. 75–7)

at which point Lear enters *'fantastically dressed with wild flowers'*

49

(IV. vi. 80). His own detachment and disorientation is also by now complete:

> Ha! Goneril, with a white beard! They flattered me like a dog, and told me I had the white hairs in my beard ere the black ones were there. To say 'aye' and 'no' to every thing that I said . . . Go to, they are not men o' their words: they told me I was every thing; 'tis a lie, I am not ague-proof.

> (IV. vi. 97–108)

and despite his claims to be

> every inch a king:
> When I do stare, see how the subject quakes.

> (IV. vi. 110–11)

there can be little doubt that this is no longer the case. This king, too, is unemployed, massively redundant, a 'ruined piece of nature'. Madness and blindness seem to have subverted the relationship of human senses and the world over which he ruled has been turned upside down:

> A man may see how this world goes with no eyes. Look with thine ears: see how yond justice rails upon yond simple thief. Hark, in thine ear: change places, and, handy-dandy, which is the justice, which is the thief?

> (IV. vi. 151–6)

The only proper response is tears, the only appropriate image, once again, that of the theatre:

> LEAR. If thou wilt weep my fortunes, take my eyes;
>   I know thee well enough; thy name is Gloucester;
>   Thou must be patient; we came crying hither:
>   Thou know'st the first time that we smell the air
>   We wawl and cry. I will preach to thee: mark.
> GLOUCESTER. Alack, alack the day!
> LEAR. When we are born, we cry that we are come
>   To this great stage of fools.

> (IV. vi. 178–85)

At the end of one world, perhaps all that remains for those left unemployed is to speak of birth.

8

Something from Nothing

That which is born out of Lear's experience takes us back to the play's beginning. Cordelia's refusal of his world of quantity and calculation had been met by the exasperated proposal that, 'Nothing will come of nothing: speak again.' But human beings never simply 'speak'. Any utterance is always complicated, particularly in a pre-literate society, by the body. Its unignorable presence supplies a living and modifying context for the voice in all face-to-face communication. Drama is the art which is made out of that.

Lear's insistence upon explicit verbal statement, through words alone, thus confirms the reductive mode of his world-view – one which is utterly unable to cope with dimensions of experience lying beyond the reach of the straightforwardly expressible. In such a world, silence, or the use of non-verbal or 'kinesic' modes of communication as adjuncts to, or modifiers of, meaning, seems merely uncommunicative. Cordelia's sense that 'my love's | More ponderous than my tongue' (I. i. 77–8), that she cannot, accordingly, 'heave | My heart into my mouth' (I. i. 91–2), and her resolve to 'Love, and be silent' (I. i. 62) meet only blank incomprehension, and later fury, by comparison with her sisters' facile wordiness.

The play virtually insists on the point. Cordelia's silence is Shakespeare's own addition to the story. Part of its purpose is to demonstrate the limitations Lear imposes on language by his commitment to words as the sole carriers of meaning. Words, after all, can be slippery. To use the terms proposed by the Swiss linguist Ferdinand de Saussure, the nature of the linguistic sign, or the word, depends upon the relationship between the two aspects of 'concept' and 'sound-image', or 'signified' and 'signifier', which constitute it. The overall characteristic of this relationship is that it is arbitrary. There is no essential or necessary 'fitness' in the connection between the sound-image made by the word 'tree' (i.e. the signifier), the concept of a tree (i.e. the signified), and the actual material tree which grows up out of the earth. Thus the linguistic sign 'tree' has no natural, or 'tree-like' qualities by which its efficacy can be judged, and there is no appeal open to a 'reality' beyond the structure of the English language in order to justify our use of it.

The result is that the 'meaning' of any word is not automatically stable, guaranteed by nature, or by the 'way things are', in what we like to call the 'real world'. That only appears to be the case. The truth is that in the 'real world' words do not always transmit the same meaning for everybody and that any agreed meaning – certainly for important words – is always a matter of social, moral, or political negotiation. Final agreement may never be possible. Our newspapers tell us every day that this is currently the case with words such as 'woman', 'democracy', 'freedom', 'family', 'terrorist', 'patriot'. We have seen the same process in operation in *King Lear* in respect of the negotiations around the very crucial word 'love'. Lear's simplistic reduction of that word's manifold dimensions finally drags him into the tragically reduced equation by whose light his own punishment will be finally calculated: 'Nothing will come of nothing.' But only a mind which persists in linking 'something' with explicit verbal protestation – dependent on words alone – could see that as an adequate response to the different realities with which his daughters confront him.

The pun on 'love' with which *King Lear* begins thus has a crucial function in the play which continues – sometimes evidently, sometimes by implication – to operate throughout the whole of the text. This is true to such a degree that it is salutary to remind ourselves at this stage that punning has only relatively recently come to be regarded as a not particularly demanding or portentous form of wit. That, needless to say, is the prejudice of a modern, literate culture. In a pre-literate community, dependent on the sound of the human voice and the physical presence of the body, the pun enjoys considerable status, because it depends precisely upon face-to-face inflection or gesture to indicate the homonym, something which language in its written form cannot allow for. This pushes the potential 'slippage' between signified and signifier – always open to exploitation in any human situation – very firmly into the foreground.

Because it utilizes that slippage, because it foregrounds the signifying processes at large, and because this enables it to press 'beyond' the limits of the simple word which generates it, the pun seems almost to embody language's capacity to overleap itself, to subvert – and in so doing to enlarge – the ordinary business of 'meaning'. In this sense, the pun exemplifies the signifying use language often makes of things that appear, to rational thinking, to be merely unfortunate, scandalous, or catastrophic. Puns, that is to say, like jokes, digressions, nods, winks, gestures, are a serious business, and any reader of the poems and sermons of the early modern period can confirm that the gravity of important matters was frequently reinforced by such means.

King Lear is no exception. And in fact it is hardly a surprise to discover that – like 'love' – the crucial word 'nothing' has a capacity for serious punning which the play exploits. Its homonym is the term 'noting'. Since 'noting' refers (via the sense of intense observation, or even that of musical sound) precisely to a range and mode of perception to which the non-verbal, non-discursive sign – beyond the reach of words – appeals, these homonyms seem almost to enact, even to affirm, the committed pre-literate orality on which they depend, and to which they are addressed. In *King Lear*'s case, what is clearly at stake in the 'nothing/noting' nexus is the range of meaning that lies beyond the reach of explicit, rational words. The play looks, as it were, into that silence which Cordelia insists is a valid expression of her love. Were Lear able to 'note' that, it seems to say, he would indeed be capable of following Kent's injunction to him to 'See better, Lear', (I. i. 158).

Cordelia's verbal withdrawal in the division scene is, therefore, not the wholesale rejection of communication that Lear takes it to be. The body, after all, talks. In fact, it is of the essence of drama itself, as well as of oral communication at large, that we take up the responsibility to 'note' the body's 'kinesic' contribution as an adjunct to and a moderation of whatever words say. This aspect of language had already perhaps received one of its clearest definitions in an earlier play of Shakespeare's whose very title embodies the pun. In *Much Ado About Nothing*, the capacity to 'note' the silent dimensions of communication turns out to be crucial to the story. In fact, the inability of Hero's accusers to 'note' beyond the level of mere words is the basis of the false accusations that lead almost to tragedy. Only the Friar, who has 'noted' her correctly, observing, for instance, the kinesic import of her blushing, can save Hero from disgrace and death. As he says,

> I have only silent been so long,
> And given way unto this course of fortune,
> By noting of the lady. I have mark'd
> A thousand blushing apparitions
> To start into her face, a thousand innocent shames
> In angel whiteness beat away those blushes,
> And in her eye there hath appear'd a fire
> To burn the errors that these princes hold
> Against her maiden truth.
>
> (*Much Ado About Nothing*, IV. i. 156–64)

The parallel with Lear's accusation of Cordelia is not exact. But when we move to the end of the play, and see him enter, finally, with Cordelia dead in his arms, he has very obviously outrun the limits of verbal communication, and similarities start to accrue. Cordelia's death, though ordered, was almost accidental and might have been avoided. Although he has 'kill'd the slave that was a-hanging thee' (V. iii. 274), Lear was unable to prevent the deed. He has cut down her body, and now piteously stalks the stage with it. As he throws back his head and howls (the text's 'Howl, howl, howl!' (V. iii. 257) is presumably a printer's sign hinting at the actor's extended, non-verbalized cries), he stresses the absence of linguistic forms appropriate to such a situation:

> Howl, howl, howl! O! you are men of stones:
> Had I your tongues and eyes, I'd use them so
> That heaven's vault should crack. She's gone for ever.
>
> (V. iii. 257–9)

He looks beyond language now, for evidence of life: for breath, not words, to see if that will 'mist or stain' a glass, or stir a feather, and so communicate hope. In the event, Cordelia's inert body serves to stress her particular involvement with silence, her long-standing commitment to the sphere of the non-verbal, her intricate relationship with 'nothing' that has marked her – as, in the earlier play, it did Hero – from the beginning. Lear even seems to have begun to grasp that Cordelia's 'nothing' – as always – might urgently communicate:

> Cordelia, Cordelia! stay a little. Ha!
> What is't thou say'st? Her voice was ever soft,
> Gentle and low, an excellent thing in woman.
>
> (V. iii. 271–3)

Lear's final words follow within seconds and their direction seems clear. It is away from 'nothing' and towards 'noting'. Following him, we can begin by noting that his announcement – made of Cordelia – that 'my poor fool is hang'd' (V. iii. 305) conclusively links the two thematically related functions noted above, and perhaps confirms that the parts of his daughter and the Fool may have been 'doubled' by the same actor. The rest of the speech deliberately draws attention to the body in his arms. Beginning with the unanswerable question

> No, no, no life!
> Why should a dog, a horse, a rat, have life,
> And thou no breath at all?
>
> (V. iii. 305–7)

it moves towards a famously pounding line of verse that projects itself well beyond the level of rational meaning:

> Thou'lt come no more,
> Never, never, never, never, never!
>
> (V. iii. 307–8)

Like the howls that precede it, this teeters on the edge of rational, verbal statement, virtually entering the non-discursive sphere of music (T. S. Eliot called the line 'sounding', meaning 'musical'). And then, as music does, the speech apparently inconsequentially draws us into itself and into the necessary final act of 'noting':

> Pray you, undo this button: thank you, Sir.
> Do you see this? Look on her, look, her lips,
> Look there, look there!   [*Dies.*]
>
> (V. iii. 309–11)

The words are almost banal. Lear asks Edgar or Kent to undo a button on the actor's costume. Cordelia's head, perhaps because the button was restraining it, now lolls back, confirming her death and possibly also revealing the damage done to her larynx by the hanging noose. And then, as Lear directs our attention to her lips with increasing intensity, 'Do you see this? Look on her, look, her lips, | Look there, look there!' (V. iii. 310–11), perhaps her mouth falls open.

As we stare at it, in response to Lear's clamorous urging, her lips, in their deathly rigor, may even seem about to form words. But what emerges from them is – nothing. In this situation, it is a silence that weighs far more heavily than any speech could. In death, as in life, Cordelia manages to speak without words, and proves capable of venturing beyond them. She says everything by saying – literally at last – nothing. And Lear dies, certainly noting the wordless eloquence in which her 'nothing' consists and perhaps even understanding the finally unutterable 'love' of which it may be the ultimate expression.

He invites us to do the same: to 'note' the vast non-discursive regions that lie beyond mere words, and beyond an instrumental reason which claims to master them. Such 'noting', the play implies, as the world lies in ruins about the bodies of Lear and Cordelia, might even become the basis for creating something out of nothing.

9

Instead of a Masterpiece

Most Shakespearean critics would rank *King Lear* among Shakespeare's masterpieces. Its assured position in the canon is reflected in the ease with which it finds its way on to most 'English' syllabuses throughout the world. It seems, more perhaps than any other of the Bard's works, to focus on the eternal verities, to express them with consummate skill, and in the process to communicate enduring truths about the unchanging human condition.

Yet no historicist view of the play can countenance such 'universalist' attributions of permanence, or such 'essentialist' claims to the transcendence of time, location, and way of life. It is surely questionable whether any human enterprise can operate beyond the limitations of culture and history, factors which shape all human activity. It follows, needless to say, that any judgements we make in the present must be subject to exactly the same project of contextualization as those of the past. As a result, any historicism of the kind that was discussed in Chapter 2 must finally come to recognize its rootedness in our own time and set out to situate *King Lear* within the cultural field produced by our own signifying practices. This means offering to assess our use of the play as an instrument of cultural meaning in our own society.

Any consideration of *King Lear*'s stage history before the twentieth century will immediately cast doubt on the assumption that the play is clearly and transcendentally recognizable as a 'masterpiece'. Initially performed in 1605–6, it was produced fairly regularly until the theatres closed in 1642. After their reopening at the Restoration, there are records of productions between 1662 and 1665 at Lincoln's Inn Fields in London, but the play was evidently not a favourite piece amongst Shakespeare's works.

In fact, in 1681 Nahum Tate presented a revised *King Lear* at

Dorset Garden, claiming that he had found the play 'a heap of jewels unstrung and unpolish'd'. His subsequent stringing and polishing imposed a number of 'improvements' – an odd, in fact impossible, term to use of a 'masterpiece'. In Tate's version, Edgar and Cordelia became lovers and Cordelia gained a confidante called Arante. The Fool was removed. The play also acquired a happy ending which restored Lear to his throne and arranged for Cordelia to marry Edgar. This version, with the approval of Dr Johnson and of well-known and established actors such as Garrick, Kemble, and Kean, held sway on the British stage for more than a century and a half. There was some competition between 1768 and 1773 from a version by George Colman, but this also omitted the Fool, and kept the happy ending. No attempt was made to present Shakespeare's version of the play until William Charles Macready's production which opened at Covent Garden on 25 January 1838. Even this omitted the details of Gloucester's blinding, and arranged for a fortuitous entrance by Lear to prevent the jump from the 'cliff'. Charles Lamb had announced in 1811 that the part of Lear was unactable and by the end of the century the play was widely considered unplayable. Occasional performances continued in London, climaxing in Henry Irving's production of 1892, but *King Lear* was not regularly produced until the twentieth century, a major landmark being Lewis Casson's production in 1940 at the Old Vic Theatre, which starred John Gielgud as Lear.

In respect of literary criticism, the story is a similar one. Though Dr Johnson judged *King Lear* to be 'deservedly celebrated', he would hardly have bestowed the accolade of 'masterpiece', finding the death of Cordelia 'contrary to the natural ideas of justice, to the hope of the reader, and, what is yet more strange, to the faith of the chronicles'. He also declared himself unimpressed by Edgar's account of the view from the cliff at Dover, and thought the blinding of Gloucester 'an act too horrid to be endured in dramatic exhibition, and such as must always compel the mind to relieve its distress by incredulity'. He added that 'I was many years ago shocked by Cordelia's death, that I know not whether I ever endured to read again the last scenes of the play till I undertook to revise them as an editor'.

Charles Lamb was more scathing: 'to see an old man tottering about the stage with a walking-stick, turned out of doors by his daughters in a rainy night, has nothing in it but what is painful and disgusting', and, while Coleridge and Hazlitt both admired the play a great deal, Thackeray found it 'a bore' in performance, even though he recognized that 'it is almost blasphemy to say that a play of Shakespeare's is bad'. The great Russian novelist Tolstoy was less cautious, concluding that *King Lear* did nothing to allay the 'repulsion, weariness and bewilderment' that Shakespeare's works usually aroused in him. He was prepared to go even further: 'far from its being the height of perfection, it is a very bad, carelessly composed production which, if it could have been of interest to a certain public at a certain time, cannot evoke amongst us anything but aversion and weariness.'

If this were not disconcerting enough, a further problem facing anyone who wishes to propose *King Lear* as an evident, established, and coherent 'masterpiece' is the existence of more than one version of the play. There is the Quarto version published in 1608, known as Q1, or the 'Pide Bull Quarto'. And then there is the version published in the First Folio collection of Shakespeare's plays in 1623. These are by no means the same text. For instance, the Folio contains 100 lines that are not in the Quarto, and the Quarto contains 300 lines that are not in the Folio. There are also a number of structural differences and emphases. For years scholars have argued about the respective claims to authority of each text, and an entirely credible hypothesis exists to the effect that the Quarto represents an initial version of the play, with the Folio offering Shakespeare's own revision of that. But a central and disturbing question still remains: which of these two versions is the 'original' or 'authoritative' one? The earlier version obviously lacks the author's mature reflections, and so perhaps it is not 'authoritative'. But to what extent can the later one claim to be 'original'? Each lacks lines that we might be sorry to lose. In practice, the text of *King Lear* that most students encounter is usually a conflation of both. But that effectively constitutes a *third* version of the play – one which would obviously have been unknown to its contemporary audience. The decision of the editors of the *Oxford Shakespeare* in 1986 to publish both versions, side by side, boldly admitted the 'problem', but scarcely solved it.

In other words, *King Lear* turns out to be a text whose history, in terms of stage performance, critical response, and its own material existence, quite clearly lacks the sort of continuing identity and coherence that we expect great works of art to have.

Their absence raises some crucial questions. If the play genuinely is a 'masterpiece', then why was it not universally perceived to be such, virtually until the late twentieth century? Can it really be the case that, for three hundred years or so, a considerable number of dramatists, poets, theatrical directors, and literary critics (some of them, obviously enough, gifted and perceptive artists of considerable distinction) were blind to its self-evident merits – merits that are suddenly quite clear to today's otherwise not especially gifted readers and theatre-goers? Does the average twentieth-century student of the play really possess more acute powers of discrimination than Dr Johnson, or Tolstoy? Is he or she better able to discern true poetic value than the person who cut out from each version some of the play's finest lines – that is, Shakespeare himself? And, in any case, which of the three versions of the play *is* the 'masterpiece'?

I have of course angled these questions unfairly, but I have done so in order to focus attention on some of the absurdities inherent in claims made for *King Lear*'s permanent and universal 'greatness'; that is, its capacity to speak meaningfully and for all time to and about an unchanging 'human nature' trapped in an enduring 'condition'. However, I also hope that, so angled, they may be able to throw into relief a particular stance which might begin to generate satisfactory answers to them.

Its fundamental principles can be briefly and baldly stated. There is no 'original', essential, unchanging *King Lear*. There is no final 'play itself' to which we can at last turn, when all the different readings of it are done. There is no 'original' text which Shakespeare uncomplicatedly thought up, and wrote down, which remains always the same, and to which access is immediate and complete, regardless of time, place, or specific circumstance. That is, there is no 'ideal' *King Lear*.

What does exist is a material object, or set of objects, on which we can and do operate in order to produce a range of 'meanings' in aspects of which our society from time to time chooses to invest. The shift of emphasis involved here is crucial: it moves our attention from a concern with sameness to a concern with difference. That is, it abandons an idealized notion of an unchanging super-being called 'Shakespeare' who bequeathed us permanent masterpieces which speak to and derive from our enduring nature. In its place, it sets the proposition that all of us

61

– even 'Shakespeare' – of necessity have our being in the flow of time called 'history', a situation whose main effect is to impose change and so differences upon us. To accept this alteration of emphasis is to propose that to some degree it is *we* who 'produce' *King Lear*, *we* who 'construct' it in whatever form the prejudices and pressures of our own time dictate. We, to that extent, and to stretch the point, for the sake of argument, almost to absurdity, are not far from being effectively the 'authors' of the play. As a result, the question 'what does *King Lear* mean?' makes much less sense than the more appropriate 'what do *we* mean *by King Lear*?'.

It should be made clear that 'we' here does not refer to us as individual beings. The argument is not that each of us constructs our own individual *King Lear* for our own individual purposes: far from it. 'We' refers to our culture at large, our way of life, the collective view of the world our society has arrived at and agreed upon in a particular place at a particular time. That notion of 'we' allows us to generalize about societies in a way that might begin to explain why a *King Lear* in the eighteenth century is something very different from a *King Lear* in the twentieth century and why, most importantly, neither of them can claim to be the 'real' or the 'right' one. There is, in this view, no such thing as the 'real' or the 'right' version of the play: not even 'Shakespeare's' version could make that claim.

This, of course, is a case made from a specific position and perhaps it is helpful at this stage broadly to label it a 'Cultural Materialist' one. The focus of such an approach will always, of course, be on the ways in which a play such as *King Lear* is processed by a society – whether an early modern society, an eighteenth-century one, or our own – rather than on any mythical 'play itself'. If I were now, by way of conclusion, to try to apply its principles to our own society, I would accordingly do so by focusing on those 'cultural meanings' that we currently generate by means of the play in our own historical context – meanings which can hardly be separated from our own particular perception of those generated then, in the text's historical context, which also form part of our 'reading' of the text. And this would lead me to ask questions concerning the gradual changes in the fortunes of *King Lear* chronicled above.

The most significant of these seem to follow the Second World War. Why is it that, in 1947, George Orwell felt able to denounce

Tolstoy's account of Lear as 'a prolonged exercise in mis-representation'? My answer might begin by focusing on the war and its aftermath. It would suggest, perhaps, that this was no ordinary conflict but one which raised for the first time the possibility of universal cataclysm by means of nuclear weapons. In addition, it had seen, in the discovery of the Nazi concentration camps, evidence of a holocaust which signalled the destruction, not only of European Jewish life, but of any idea that European civilization itself might present something of permanent value to the world. The horrors revealed in 1944–5 indicated the persistence of a barbarism – and in a nation widely judged to mark the high point of European civilization before the arrival of the Nazi regime – that most had thought long vanished.

The war also brought the collapse of another world. The US President, Franklin Roosevelt, had made it quite clear that the price of the United States' entry into the European conflict was that the British should give up their Empire. The result of its demise was that the balance of the world decisively shifted. The United States took over from the British the role of premier Western power and a US general was duly made Supreme Commander of Allied forces and given charge of the D-Day operation. Prime Minister Harold Macmillan's plaintive 'These Americans represent the new Roman Empire and we Britons, like the Greeks of old, must teach them how to make it go' may rank as mere whistling in the dark, but it shows how impenetrable that dark was.

All of these experiences – the shattering of worlds, the holocaust, the loss of Empire – suggest a climate in which *King Lear* might climb urgently to the top of a list of Shakespeare's plays, there to be constructed as a masterpiece of universal destruction and decline which had particular relevance to the British Isles. Orwell argues that Tolstoy found the play intolerable because the story of Lear's situation had many resemblances to the Russian's own: 'The subject of *Lear* is renunciation . . . Lear renounces his throne but expects everyone to continue treating him as a king. He does not see that if he surrenders power, other people will take advantage of his weakness . . .'[1] However, in the terms in which Orwell casts it, Lear's situation has just as many resemblances to the plight of post-war Britain.

Such an account of the play might seem merely practical, in a traditional British mode, at best only of so-called 'academic' interest. But it can also reasonably claim to have broader horizons. In focusing on the way in which different readings of texts compete for the power to generate cultural meaning, and in aiming to see how ideological positions are formed and sustained through their use; how, more specifically, discursive stratagems operate in the criticism and performance of Shakespeare's plays, and on behalf of what and of whom, this sort of analysis commits itself to intervention in matters traditionally thought to lie beyond the walls of the academy. Add an overt concern with the material historical and economic implications of literary criticism itself, together with a focus on the relation between the academic subject called 'English' and the cultural power of the Englishness which it often upholds, and the sense of this kind of criticism's involvement, at its furthest reach, with larger matters of politics and public policy is unavoidable.

The plainest of facts is that most people encounter *King Lear* as part of the academic subject called 'English', and that context is a far from neutral one. For the British, 'English' never was and never could be just another academic subject. On the contrary, its larger dimension grows directly out of the fact that it was always intended to be *the* subject, both at home and, with perhaps greater significance, abroad: the sacred repository of national values, standards, and identity; the crucible in which a whole way of life was to be reverently concocted, shaken, and occasionally stirred. 'English' had a missionary function, both at home and abroad, from its very inception. And yet, as recent and continuing stirrings amongst non-English communities in Britain have shown, those on the periphery of this civilizing arrangement, the non-civilized or Brutish, have a disconcerting habit of periodically dashing that cup from English lips. In the process, perhaps, they remind us of the complexity of our inheritance from Brutus, to which *King Lear* glancingly refers.

A literary criticism which responds – beyond the boundaries of 'English' – to those peripheral Brutish dimensions might not unreasonably, as I have already suggested, find a sort of rallying-point in the work of the late Raymond Williams – a Welshman from the periphery, not an Englishman from the centre, with a lifelong interest in mapping those dimensions of the boundary-ridden British terrain which his finest novel calls *Border*

Country. To such a criticism, all texts will ultimately speak, not of their essential meaning or aesthetic being, but in more mundane social and political terms of the uses to which they have been and may be put. But it would be misleading, as well as clearly against the fundamental tenets of this sort of approach, to suggest that the project is watertight, complete, and devoid of serious difficulties. Far from it. If Cultural Materialism, for instance, were not itself permanently in process, it would have been overtaken by a serious contradiction. The problems any such programmes face are many, and, amongst others, the following seem of particular importance.

First, the position from which both New Historicism and Cultural Materialism argue risks being compromised by aspects of the argument itself. Thus, if all cultures can and must be 'historicized' and if their natures and concerns ultimately turn out to be unwittingly tailored to and unconsciously imprisoned by the economic, social, and political pressures of their age and their way of life, then so is our own. Future historians will have no trouble demonstrating that, far from at last presenting the 'truth' about Shakespearian drama, both New Historicism and Cultural Materialism are enterprises which, as products of our current Western European or North American presuppositions, prove to be as blindly culture-specific as the societies they describe. However, this is only a disabling factor if we persist in regarding the attainment of permanent, transhistorical truth as the object of the exercise. If we abandon that goal, then, once the limitations of both methods are recognized, they become aspects of a self-knowledge which valuably sharpens the process of reading and even helps the reader towards a more telling purchase on its purpose in the current and continuing debate concerning the construction and reconstruction of our own world.

Second, as part of their project of seeking out precise moments of potential contradiction and subversion, both New Historicists and Cultural Materialists have to argue that what they observe has an objective and positive existence in Elizabethan society, and is not merely the product of a particular mode of reading. This seems to be a path which might ultimately lead to the mere replacement of one invented 'Elizabethan World Picture' by another. The position is again partly retrievable to the extent that Cultural Materialism's motives are at least clear. Its final interest in the use we make of Shakespeare in our own world is usually firmly declared. And that makes all the difference in so far as its aim is thus not simply to describe the past 'as it was'. It is, rather, polemically to reread, renarrate, and so reclaim the past in the name of the construction of a more acceptable present.

Third, for a culture to exist at all, and to be meaningful to itself, it will always need to establish principles of subordination, and marginalization. Not all voices in any society can claim an equal right to be heard. Is not the idea of pluralism, or the wholesale abandonment of exclusion – sometimes seemingly advocated by Cultural Materialism – therefore merely sentimental? Can it not be asked of any text in any culture, whose voice is being silenced in order that it may speak? Is it enough for the Cultural Materialist critic to expose the relation of dominant and subordinated or silenced voices? Is not some imperative also implied? And does this not land us ultimately with the problem of moral choice? Do we not finally have to choose which voices are to be silenced? If the answer to these questions is yes, it can only be justified on the understanding that the question will be repeatedly asked, that the answer will be regularly scrutinized, and that the sort of cultural interrogation it implies will be constantly carried out. Cultural Materialism, or New Historicism, or indeed any sort of historicist Shakespearian criticism worth its salt ought, in some degree, to be a guarantor of that sort of vigilance. As I have said elsewhere, its voice is one of those we might hope to hear whenever the latest King Lear, striding on to the stage, calls ominously for a map to be brought before him.

Notes

CHAPTER 2. USING HISTORY

1. Leonard Tennenhouse, *Power on Display: The Politics of Shakespeare's Genres* (London: Routledge, 1986), 10.
2. Hugh Grady, *The Modernist Shakespeare* (Oxford: Oxford University Press, 1991), 225–35.
3. Jonathan Dollimore and Alan Sinfield (eds.), *Political Shakespeare: New Essays in Cultural Materialism* (Manchester: Manchester University Press, 1985), p. viii.
4. Terence Hawkes, *Meaning by Shakespeare* (London: Routledge, 1992), 1–10.
5. Raymond Williams, *Marxism and Literature* (Oxford: Oxford University Press, 1977), 121–7.
6. Jonathan Dollimore, 'Critical Developments: Cultural Materialism, Feminism and Gender Critique, and New Historicism', in Stanley Wells (ed.), *Shakespeare: A Bibliographical Guide* (Oxford: Oxford University Press, 1990), 414.
7. Jonathan Dollimore, 'Shakespeare, Cultural Materialism, Feminism and Marxist Humanism', *New Literary History*, 21 (1989–90), 472.
8. See Dollimore and Sinfield (eds.) *Political Shakespeare*, p. viii.

CHAPTER 4. BEING REASONABLE

1. There are various accounts of the notion of 'instrumental reason'. See Jurgen Habermas, *Knowledge and Human Interests*, trans. Jeremy J. Shapiro (London: Heinemann, 1972); Theodore W. Adorno and Max Horkheimer, *Dialectic of Enlightenment*, trans. John Cumming (London: Routledge, 1972); and Max Weber, *Economy and Society*, ed. Gunther Roth and Claus Wittich (Berkeley, Calif.: University of California Press, 1978).

CHAPTER 5. REASON AND MADNESS: MALE AND FEMALE

1. See Coppelia Kahn, *Man's Estate: Masculine Identity in Shakespeare* (Berkeley, Calif,: California University Press, 1981), 11. These and other views are subjected to a careful critique by Kathleen McLuskie in 'The Patriarchal Bard: Feminist Criticism and Shakespeare: *King Lear* and *Measure for Measure*', in Dollimore and Sinfield (eds.), *Political Shakespeare*, 88–108.
2. Coppelia Kahn, 'The Absent Mother in *King Lear*', in Margaret Ferguson, Maureen Quilligan, and Nancy Vickers (eds.), *Rewriting the Renaissance: The Discourses of Sexual Difference in Early Modern Europe* (Chicago: University of Chicago Press, 1986), 33–49, at p. 36: Mary Beth Rose, 'Where are the Mothers in Shakespeare? Options for Gender Representation in the English Renaissance', *Shakespeare Quarterly*, 42 (Fall 1991), 291–314, at pp. 301–2, 307, 312.
3. One such reading is Marilyn French, *Shakespeare's Division of Experience* (London: Cape, 1982). For an account of its shortcomings, see McLuskie, 'The Patriarchal Bard'.
4. See McLuskie, 'The Patriarchal Bard', 92.

CHAPTER 6. MASTERLESS MEN

1. See Christopher Hill, 'Masterless Men', in *The World Turned Upside Down* (Harmondsworth: Penguin Books, 1975), 39–56; also A. L. Beier, *Masterless Men: The Vagrancy Problem in England 1560–1640* (London: Routledge, 1985).

CHAPTER 7. ROLES AND GOALS

1. Marshall McLuhan, *The Gutenberg Galaxy: The Making of Typographic Man* (London: Routledge, 1962), 14–18.

CHAPTER 9. INSTEAD OF A MASTERPIECE

1. George Orwell, 'Lear, Tolstoy and the Fool', *Polemic*, 7 (Mar., 1947). See *The Collected Essays, Journalism and Letters of George Orwell* ed. Sonia Orwell and Ian Angus (Harmondsworth: Penguin Books, 1970), 340.

Select Bibliography

The amount of material currently being produced on Shakespeare is both alarming and revealing. What follows can only be a tentative guide. However, its glance at the outline of one of the most amazing monuments ever erected by human beings may prompt thoughts about the ideological force of the notion of 'universal genius'. See above, Chapter 9. This selection of items reflects the prejudices made clear in the arguments that precede it, but it is offered in the hope that wider reading may result in some of them being modified.

Note: With a few necessary exceptions, items in the various sections are arranged in chronological order.

EDITIONS OF *King Lear*

There are a number of useful and reasonably priced single-volume editions of the play. All of them consist of a conflation of the Quarto and the Folio texts (see above, Chapter 9). The following are most widely available:

Fraser, Russell (ed.), *King Lear* (Signet Classic Shakespeare; New York: New American Library, 1963).
Hunter, G. K. (ed.), *King Lear* (New Penguin Shakespeare; Harmondsworth: Penguin Books, 1972).
Muir, Kenneth (ed.), *King Lear* (Arden Shakespeare; London: Methuen (Routledge), 1952; rev. 1985).
Halio, Jay L. (ed.), *The Tragedy of King Lear* (New Cambridge Shakespeare; Cambridge: Cambridge University Press, 1992).

The most significant textual development in recent years undoubtedly springs from the decision of the editors of the Oxford Shakespeare to publish the Quarto and Folio versions of the play side by side.

Wells, Stanley, and Taylor, Gary (eds.), *William Shakespeare: The Complete Works* (Oxford: Oxford University Press, 1986). See above, Chapter 9.

On the textual question

Stone, P. W. K., *The Textual History of King Lear* (London: Scolar Press, 1980).

Urkowitz, Steven, *Shakespeare's Revision of King Lear* (Princeton, NJ: Princeton University Press, 1980).

Blayney, Peter W. M., *The Texts of King Lear and their Origins* (Cambridge: Cambridge University Press, 1982).

Taylor, Gary, and Warren, Michael (eds.), *The Division of the Kingdoms: Shakespeare's Two Versions of King Lear* (Oxford: Clarendon Press, 1983).

Goldberg, Jonathan, 'Textual Properties', *Shakespeare Quarterly*, 37/2 (summer 1986), 213–17. Discusses some of the theoretical implications of *King Lear*'s textual history.

NEW THEORIES OF SHAKESPEARIAN CRITICISM

The criticism of Shakespeare has always been central to the academic study of the subject called 'English Literature'. The impact of recent theoretical developments in this area has been powerful, with consequential effects on the subject at large. Some of the most significant developments of recent years are represented below. 'New Historicism' and 'Cultural Materialism' feature strongly (see above, Chapter 2), but broader considerations have also been taken into account, such as the place of history in the study of Shakespeare, the 'use' of Shakespeare in the construction of cultural meaning, Shakespeare and 'English', and Shakespearian texts as an aspect of ideology.

Some introductory surveys

Dollimore, Jonathan, 'Shakespeare, Cultural Materialism, Feminism and Marxist Humanism', *New Literary History*, 21 (1989–90), 471–93.

——'Critical Developments', in Stanley Wells (ed.), *Shakespeare: A Bibliographical Guide* (Oxford: Oxford University Press, 1990), 405–28.

Grady, Hugh, *The Modernist Shakespeare* (Oxford: Oxford University Press, 1991). Perhaps the most incisive overall survey of the origins of New Historicism and Cultural Materialism, and of their relation to the broader twentieth-century critical and ideological terrain.

Collections of essays

Dollimore, Jonathan, and Sinfield, Alan (eds.), *Political Shakespeare: New Essays in Cultural Materialism* (Manchester: Manchester University Press, 1985). This is the volume which, in general terms, first proposed the fundamental concepts of 'Cultural Materialism'. See, especially, Jonathan Dollimore's introductory essay, 'Shakespeare, Cultural Materialism and the New Historicism', pp. 2–17.

Drakakis, John (ed.), *Alternative Shakespeares* (London: Routledge, 1985). A more broadly ranging collection, no less ground-breaking than the above, and published in the same year. Containing work by Christopher Norris, Catherine Belsey, Malcolm Evans, and others, it was designed as part of the 'New Accents' series – volumes aiming specifically to introduce new critical developments in 'English' and related subjects.

Parker, Patricia, and Hartman, Geoffrey (eds.), *Shakespeare and the Question of Theory* (London and New York: Methuen, 1985). An important collection: amongst others, the essays by Howard Felperin and Stanley Cavell are notable examples of close reading sharpened by philosophical considerations.

Atkins, G. Douglas, and Bergeron, David M. (eds.), *Shakespeare and Deconstruction* (New York: Peter Lang, 1988). The title speaks for itself. See, particularly, Jackson I. Cope, 'Shakespeare, Derrida and the End of Language', pp. 267–83, and Jonathan Goldberg, 'Perspectives: Dover Cliff and the Conditions of Representation', pp. 245–56 – both excellent examples of the disconcerting power of deconstructive analysis.

Individual works of specific interest

Dollimore, Jonathan, *Radical Tragedy: Religion, Ideology and Power in the Drama of Shakespeare and his Contemporaries* (Brighton: Harvester, 1984; rev. 1990). A ground-breaking work which stresses the link between drama and political power in the early modern period. See, in particular, the chapter '*King Lear* and Essentialist Humanism', pp. 189–203. This is reprinted in John Drakakis (ed.), *Shakespearean Tragedy* (Longman Critical Readers; London: Longman, 1992), 194–208.

Evans, Malcolm, *Signifying Nothing* (Brighton: Harvester, 1988; rev. edn. 1990). An explosively entertaining and unsettlingly witty account of Shakespeare in the light of recent theories of subjectivity, signification, and ideology.

Belsey, Catherine, *The Subject of Tragedy* (London: Routledge, 1985). Deals, amongst other matters, with the rise of the individual 'subject' in early modern ideology, the social conflicts at stake, and the impact of these on the drama.

Sinfield, Alan, *Faultlines: Cultural Materialism and the Politics of Dissident Reading* (Oxford: Oxford University Press, 1992). A wide-ranging collection of essays exploring the issue of how dissident reading can disrupt the interpretation of texts, some of them Shakespearian.

Howard, Jean E., *The Stage and Social Struggle in Early Modern England* (London: Routledge, 1994). Firmly locates the theatre in its social and political context and asesses its role in the class, gender, and sexual conflicts of the time.

The 'use' of Shakespeare

Hawkes, Terence, *That Shakespeherian Rag* (London: Routledge, 1986).

——*Meaning by Shakespeare* (London: Routledge, 1992). In a sense, these are companion volumes, although they can be approached separately. The essay 'Lear's Maps' in *Meaning by Shakespeare* forms the basis of the arguments in Chapters 2 and 9 above. In the same volume, 'Bardbiz' reviews the books – amongst others – of Gary Taylor and Michael D. Bristol, mentioned below.

Holderness, Graham, and McCullough, Christopher (eds.), *The Shakespeare Myth* (Manchester: Manchester University Press, 1987). Contains valuable investigations of the growth of a national monument.

Howard, Jean E., and O'Connor, Marion F. (eds.), *Shakespeare Reproduced: The Text in History and Ideology* (London: Routledge 1988). Contains come incisive probing of the whole idea of 'reproduction' in culture, and of the implication of 'Shakespeare' in the process; see, especially, Walter Cohen, 'Political Criticism of Shakespeare', pp. 18–46.

Taylor, Gary, *Reinventing Shakespeare* (London: The Hogarth Press, 1990). An amusing, scholarly, and vastly informative account of how each age invents and invests in its own 'Shakespeare' for its own purposes (see above, Chapter 9).

Bristol, Michael D., *Shakespeare's America: America's Shakespeare* (London: Routledge, 1990). The creation of 'Shakespeare' as an American institution, and the workings of the cultural and ideological productive forces involved.

Radical Marxist–Humanist approaches

Eagleton, Terry, *William Shakespeare* (Oxford: Blackwell, 1986). A brief but important, witty, and on occasion deliberately 'shocking' study.

Ryan, Kiernan, *Shakespeare* (Harvester 'New Readings' series; Brighton: Harvester, 1989). Also brief, but offers a valuable confrontation with other 'historicist' approaches.

Margolies, David, *Monsters of the Deep: Social Dissolution in Shakespeare's Tragedies* (Manchester: Manchester University Press, 1992). Gives a powerful account of the impact of individualism on the social order in *King Lear* (see above, Chapter 3).

New Historicism

Howard, Jean E., 'The New Historicism in Renaissance Studies', *English Literary Renaissance*, 16 (1986), 13–43. An early, but highly influential survey which clarifies and summarizes the issues most effectively.

Veeser, H. Aram (ed.), *The New Historicism* (London: Routledge, 1990). A useful collection of essays, with an introduction.

——(ed.), *The New Historicism Reader* (London: Routledge, 1994). A collection of key writings by some of the prime movers in the field.

Thomas, Brook, *The New Historicism* (Princeton, NJ: Princeton University Press, 1991). A useful, sometimes challenging introduction.

Greenblatt, Stephen, *Renaissance Self-Fashioning* (Chicago: Chicago, University Press, 1980). Greenblatt is the leading American New Historicist. Not primarily concerned with Shakespeare, this was the first of his works to attract the 'New Historicist' label, although it was by no means self-inflicted. See the three introductory items above.

——*Shakespearean Negotiations: The Circulation of Social Energy in Renaissance England* (Oxford: Clarendon Press, 1988). An elegant and provocative study. The essay 'Shakespeare and the Exorcists', pp. 94–128, is of particular interest in respect of *King Lear*.

——*Learning to Curse: Essays in Early Modern Culture* (London: Routledge, 1991). The essay 'The Cultivation of Anxiety: King Lear and his Heirs', pp. 80–98, is a particularly striking example of one of New Historicism's most effective manœuvres, whereby the insertion of a literary text into a broader context – often using an anecdote for the purpose – suddenly and surprisingly expands its range.

Tennenhouse, Leonard, *Power on Display: The Politics of Shakespeare's Genres* (London: Routledge, 1986). A perceptive and innovative New Historicist analysis which sees the early modern theatre as a cultural forum for staging displays of political power.

Gender relations

Lenz, Carolyn; Swift, Ruth; Greene, Gayle; Neely, Carol Thomas (eds.), *The Woman's Part: Feminist Criticism of Shakespeare* (Urbana, Ill.: Illinois University Press, 1980). Probably the best general introduction to the field; the three following works are more specialized.

Kahn, Coppelia, *Man's Estate: Masculine Identity in Shakespeare* (Berkeley, Calif.: California University Press, 1981).

Novy, Marianne, *Love's Argument: Gender Relations in Shakespeare* (Chapel Hill, NC: University of North Carolina Press, 1984).

Erickson, Peter, *Patriarchal Studies in Shakespeare's Drama* (Berkeley, Calif., and London: University of California Press, 1985). See especially pp. 103–15.

STUDIES OF *King Lear*

Bradley, A. C., *Shakespearean Tragedy* (London: Macmillan, 1904; repr. 1978 and subsequently). The classic turn-of-the-century account of Shakespeare's tragedies, which, notwithstanding a host of acutely intelligent observations, virtually makes the plays over into Victorian novels. Nevertheless, its world-wide influence remains astonishingly strong, despite the brilliance of L. C. Knights's devastating attack 'How Many Children Had Lady Macbeth?', made in 1933 and reprinted in his *Explorations* (London: Chatto, 1946), 13–50. The stance Bradley adopts still seems the 'natural' and 'obvious' one to large numbers of people. It does so to an extent that suggests it may ultimately connect with deep-lying dimensions of Western ideology, thus making it virtually 'invisible'. In far too many educational settings, this highly theorized, highly partial study is still presented as open-handed and theory-free; an example of 'pure' Shakespearian 'criticism itself'. See Terence Hawkes, *That Shakespeherean Rag*, 27–50, and Hugh Grady, *The Modernist Shakespeare*, both mentioned above. (Also see above, Chapters 4 and 9).

Knight, G. Wilson, *The Wheel of Fire: Interpretations of Shakespearean Tragedy* (London: Methuen, 1930; rev. edn., 1949). One of the first, and deservedly most famous, of the 'modernist' versions of *King Lear* (to use Hugh Grady's term; see his *The Modernist Shakespeare* above). Enormously influential, it broke entirely away from A. C. Bradley's quasi-realistic, psychologically centred 'character' criticism, to present the play as a non-naturalistic 'thematic' creation, structured more like a poem than a novel (see above, Chapter 4).

Shakespeare Survey 13 (Cambridge: Cambridge University Press, 1960) and *Shakespeare Survey 33* (Cambridge: Cambridge University Press, 1980) have been devoted to *King Lear*.

Mack, Maynard, *King Lear in our Time* (Berkeley, Calif.: University of California Press, 1965). Amongst other concerns, puts the case that the horrors of two world wars, and particularly revelations concerning the concentration camps, have made *King Lear* the central Shakespearian play for the twentieth century (see above, Chapter 9).

McLuhan, Marshall, *The Gutenberg Galaxy: The Making of Typographic Man*

(London: Routledge, 1962). Pages 11–18 of this remarkable book offer a startling picture of *King Lear* as a text poised on the brink of the modern world, and constitute a brief but brilliant insight into the nature of the play and its potential meaning for the twentieth century. Compare Jonathan Goldberg's essay, 'Perspectives: Dover Cliff and the Conditions of Representation', in G. Douglas Atkins and David M. Bergeron (eds.), *Shakespeare and Deconstruction* (New York: Peter Lang, 1988), mentioned above.

Colie, Rosalie, and Flahiff, F. T. (eds.), *Some Facets of King Lear: Essays in Prismatic Criticism* (Toronto and London: University of Toronto Press, 1974). A slightly dated but interesting survey of critical opinion current at the time of its publication. Martha Andresen's ' "Ripeness is All": Sententiae and Commonplaces in *King Lear*', pp. 145–68, gives a valuable sense of the play's medieval roots.

French, Marilyn, *Shakespeare's Division of Experience* (London: Cape, 1982). An early 'feminist' analysis. For an account of its shortcomings see Kathleen McLuskie's article below. (Also see above, Chapter 5.)

McLuskie, Kathleen, 'The Patriarchal Bard: Feminist Criticism and Shakespeare: *King Lear* and *Measure for Measure*', in Jonathan Dollimore and Alan Sinfield (eds.) *Political Shakespeare: New Essays in Cultural Materialism* (Manchester: Manchester University Press, 1985), 88–108 (see above, Chapter 5).

Kahn, Coppelia, 'The Absent Mother in *King Lear*', in Margaret Ferguson, Maureen Quilligan, and Nancy Vickers (eds.), *Rewriting the Renaissance: The Discourses of Sexual Difference in Early Modern Europe* (Chicago: University of Chicago Press, 1986). See above, Chapter 5.

Marcus, Leah, *Puzzling Shakespeare: Local Reading and its Discontents* (Berkeley Calif., and London: University of California Press, 1988). The section 'Retrospective: *King Lear* on St. Stephen's Night, 1606', pp. 148–59, is an excellent example of New Historical analysis, here presented as 'local reading'. In it, the play is redeemed from a false transcendence by being firmly reinserted into its contemporary 'local' context. In this case, James's project for the creation of 'Great Britain' out of the union of England and Scotland has a central role (see above, Chapter 2).

Patterson, Annabel, *Shakespeare and the Popular Voice* (Oxford: Blackwell, 1989). The chapter ' "What matter who's speaking?": *Hamlet* and *King Lear*' stresses the importance of the 'union issue' and relates it to the 'voices' of popular culture and social protest in the play (see above, Chapter 2).

Callaghan, Dympna, *Woman and Gender in Renaissance Tragedy: A Study of King Lear, Othello, The Duchess of Malfi and the White Devil* (New York and London: Harvester Wheatsheaf, 1989). See above, Chapter 5.

Rose, Mary Beth, 'Where are the Mothers In Shakespeare? Options for Gender Representation in the English Renaissance', *Shakespeare Quarterly*, 42/3 (Fall 1991), 291–314. See above, Chapter 5.

Simpson, David, 'Great Things of Us Forgot: Seeing *Lear* Better', in Colin MacCabe (ed.), *Futures for English* (Manchester: Manchester University Press, 1988), 15–31. See above, Chapter 9.

Cartwright, Kent, *Shakespearean Tragedy and its Double: The Rhythms of Audience Response* (Pennsylvania: Pennsylvania State University Press, 1991). Explores the way in which the plays manipulate their audience. In the case of *King Lear*, the significance of the act of observation itself is stressed.

Foakes, R. A., *Hamlet versus Lear, Cultural Politics and Shakespeare's Art* (Cambridge: Cambridge University Press, 1993). An interesting survey of the protracted competition between *Hamlet* and *King Lear* for primacy in the Shakespearian canon and the light this sheds on the politics of 'culture' (see above, Chapter 9).

Armstrong, Philip, 'Uncanny Spectacles: Psychoanalysis and the Texts of *King Lear*', *Textual Practice*, 8/3 (Winter 1994), 414–34. Based on concepts developed by the French psychoanalyst, Jacques Lacan.

Collections of essays

Thompson, Ann, *King Lear: The Critics Debate* (London: Macmillan, 1988). A brief but useful general survey of the field.

Ryan, Kiernan (ed.), *King Lear* (New Casebook Series; London: Macmillan, 1993). At present, the most valuable collection of essays on the play, fully reflecting recent developments in Shakespearian criticism and offering some trenchant examples.

Index

Actors, 26
Albany, 5
Albion's England, 9
Alliteration, 20, 22
Architecture, 12
Armstrong, Philip, ix

Beier, A. L., 68, n.1
Binary opposition, 13
Blindness, 33, 48–51
Brutus, 2–3
Burgundy, 1, 7

Casson, Lewis, 59
Catholics, 3
Character, 9
Christ, Jesus, 7
Cinderella, 10
Coleridge, Samuel Taylor, 60
Colman, George, 59
Contradiction, 22
Cordelia, 6–7, 9, 24, 32–40
    passim., 52–7 *passim.*, 58–60
Cornwall, 5
Cross-dressing, 15
Cultural Materialism, vii,
    11–16, 21, 62–66, *see*
    Bibliography, pp. 70–71
Culture, 14, 15
Cupid,33

Division, 23
Dollimore, Jonathan, 14–16
Doubling, 34, 56–7

Early modern period, 41–51, 62
Edgar, 9, 36, 39, 43–6 *passim.*,
    48–51, 58–9
Edmund, 10, 18–22, 36, 48–51
Eliot, T. S., 56
Elizabeth I, Queen, 2, 19
Emblematic art, 25–6
Enclosure, 45–6
English, academic subject of,
    64–6

Fathers, 37
Femaleness, 32, 35–46 *passim.*
Folk customs, 12
Fool, The, 33–40 *passim.*, 42–3,
    56–9
Foucault, Michel, 11
France, 1
French, Marilyn, 68 n.3

Garrick, 9
Gender, 35–42
Gesture, 22, 54–7
Gielgud, Sir John, 59
Gloucester, 1, 9, 17, 36–7, 43–6
    passim., 48–51, 59
Goneril, 9, 10, 19, 23, 26, 27–31,
    46, 48
Grady, Hugh, 12
Great Britain, 2, 3
Gunpowder Plot, 3, 16, 20

Hazlitt, William, 60
Henry VIII, King, 20

Memory

up left righ

2, 4, 6 8, down

* #   5 2 reveal